PSYCHOLOGICAL DIFFERENCES:

Causes, Consequences,
and Uses in
Education and Guidance

PSYCHOLOGICAL DIFFERENCES:

Causes, Consequences,
and Uses in
Education and Guidance

James A. Wakefield, Jr.
and
Nancy A. Goad

EdITS
SAN DIEGO, CALIFORNIA 92107

First Printing, April 1982

ISBN: 0-912736-27-5

Library of Congress catalog card number: LC 82-71256

CONTENTS

FIGURES

CHAPTER 1

PSYCHOLOGY AND INDIVIDUAL DIFFERENCES

During the past century, psychology has been characterized by three broad approaches. They are the verbal-descriptive approach characterized by Freud, the experimental approach founded by Wundt, and the individual differences approach dating from Galton's work in the mid-1800's. The third approach is the topic of this book. All three approaches were started during approximately the same time period—the middle and late 1800's—and all three have made substantial advances during the past century.

The approach that is most widely discussed outside academic psychology is the verbal-descriptive approach by Freud and his followers. They wrote in the tradition of the grand personality theory based on clinical insight. These writers include Freud, Jung, Adler, Horney, and more recently Rogers. There are fundamental disagreements among these theorists, and all would probably object to being included in a list with one or more of the others. Their unifying characteristic is their practice of drawing on their clinical experiences to produce general theories of human personality with few formal attempts to test these theories empirically. (It should be noted that Rogers is an exception to this statement. Having been influenced by the other approaches, he has been responsible for empirically testing his techniques, although his basic theory is probably too general to be tested.)

There are several reasons the verbal-descriptive approach is the most popular approach. First, it is associated with medicine. Freud developed his theory in his psychiatric practice and suggested that it was merely to be used until sufficient neurological information accumulated to replace it. Similarly, the other theorists mentioned have been either psychiatrists or clinical psychologists. This approach is typically the only exposure medical students (or for that matter, practicing psychiatrists) have with psychology. Medical opinions given to patients and popularized medical accounts of psychological disturbances are usually presented in Freudian or neo-Freudian terms, such as ego, superego, oepidal complex, penis envy, etc. These concepts have become widely used even if not fully believed by many of the people who use them.

In addition to the authority given to this approach by its association with medicine, the verbal-descriptive approach is popular because it can be read by literate people without technical backgrounds. The terms that must be learned to understand this approach are by now roughly understood by most educated people. Statistics, experimental controls, and data that sometimes fail to support the theory do not appear in this approach as they do in the other approaches. Although associated with medicine, only the most superficial anatomical information is referred to by these theorists.

Since this approach to psychology can be read without a technical background, it has been widely used in literary criticism. English literature students commonly analyze Freudian or Jungian symbols found in fictional works to explain the motivations and emotions of the fictional characters and their authors. As this practice becomes common, new fictional works— books, movies, television shows—use concepts from this approach as formulae for plots and character development. To the extent that people read or watch this material and model their behavior on the behavior of the fictional characters, the various theories actually become better descriptions of human behavior as human behavior becomes more similar to the theories.

Finally, this approach is popular because the theories, particularly Freud's are presented authoritatively. Unlike the other approaches, the verbal-descriptive theorists typically present only examples that are unequivocally supportive of their theories. Qualifying terms such as "often" or "tend to" do not occur as frequently as in the other approaches. In fact, it has been common to question the psychological health of persons who would not accept the authoritative statements made by various followers of this approach. Presented authoritatively, any theory in this approach can seem too comfortingly true—like one's own religion or "real" science that consists of what is already known rather than what scientists are trying to find out.

The second approach to psychology is the experimental approach. This approach dates from the 1860's in Wundt's laboratory in Germany. Less concerned with general theory and more concerned with specific, technical problems, this approach has been less generally popular, but it has dominated academic psychology during the past century. Topics such as perception and learning have occupied experimental psychologists. They have been concerned with the reactions of people (although frequently using animals such as the white rat for economic and sometimes ethical reasons) to various stimuli or environmental conditions.

The work done in the experimental approach is almost entirely done in the laboratory under controlled conditions. This allows the psychologist to observe small differences in reactions to various stimuli such as lights, sounds, food, or electric shock that would normally be difficult to observe outside the laboratory. Since many of these stimuli occur simultaneously outside the laboratory, it is impossible to determine what stimuli or combination of stimuli a person is reacting to without controlling them and presenting them systematically.

The popularity of the experimental approach has been limited by its technical presentation. Reading an experiment is, except for the few people actively working on and intensely involved in a problem, a tedious affair. Apparatus, procedures, statistics must all be considered critically since any one of them could, if not correct, product misleading results. The results themselves make reading experiments less enjoyable than they might be since usually they are not overwhelmingly supportive of the writer's ideas. Statements such as "many of the subjects performed slightly better under condition A than under condition B" do not lead to the comforting certitude that unqualified statements from authorities produce.

The use of animal subjects in some branches of experimental psychology has also contributed to the limited popularity of the approach. It is harder to identify with the experimentalist's white rat or pigeon than it is with the verbal-descriptive theorist's unhappy, confused patient. Many students of introductory psychology are disappointed by experiements involving rats rather than humans and complain that experimental psychology seems to be about rats rather than people. While using animals does cause difficulty in generalizing to people, experimental psychology is nevertheless (primarily) about people and uses animals only because there are many experiments that are too destructive, dangerous, unpleasant, prolonged, costly, or simply boring to subject people to.

The useful applications of experimental psychological research are far more prevalent than one might expect from its limited popular readership. This approach has yielded procedures for managing mental patients and facilitating education that have become almost universally applied. Contributions have also been made to optometry, industry, legal practice and many other fields. Trained animals perform a variety of acts that could only be shaped by carefully using procedures developed by experimental psychologists. In fact, the ubiquitous vending machine is a variation of the apparatus that experimental psychologists use for giving food to an animal to reward it for a particular behavior (in this case, putting money in a slot).

The third approach to psychology is the study of individual differences. Beginning with Galton's work in the middle 1800's, differential psychologists have dealt with relationships among various human characteristics such as intelligence, personality, etc., that are discussed in this book. These characteristics are used practically to predict important future behavior, such as educational success, personal adjustment, and vocational choice and success.

With regard to popularity, the study of individual differences has, for most of its history, occupied a place intermediate between the experimental approach and the verbal-descriptive approach. Largely because of research on the concept of intelligence, results of research into individual differences attracts more widespread interest than does experimental psychology, but still not as much as the verbal-descriptive writers. In fact, the popularity of research into individual differences is somewhat obscured by the willingness of these psychologists to measure concepts derived from the other approaches. Many personality characteristics first suggested by verbal-descriptive theorists have matured through the work of researchers in individual differences. Likewise, educational achievement tests used to assess the effects of experimental procedures are usually constructed by psychologists interested in individual differences.

The academic position of individual differences has usually been subordinate to one of the other approaches. In most academic psychology departments, individual differences is less well represented than experimental psychology. In medical schools, the verbal-descriptive tradition has predominated, although the impact of clinical testing has assured that some psychologists with training in individual differences will be represented. Educational and industrial psychologists are primarily trained in individual differences and contribute directly to academic departments of education and business as well as to schools and industrial settings.

The application of individual differences is primarily through testing. Tests for intelligence, achievement, vocational interests, abilities, personality, etc., are common in our lives. These are used to make a wide variety of decisions that affect us considerably. What schools we can go to, what job we can work at, and whether we can drive are a few decisions that are influenced in part by tests and research in individual differences.

Psychologists trained in each of the three approaches—verbal-descriptive, experimental, and individual differences—regard their own approach as scientific and may or may not be willing to consider the other approaches scientific. Of course, what is or is not scientific depends on exactly what definition of scientific is used. If the definition emphasizes establishing causal relationships by carefully controlled manipulation of variables, the experimental approach has the advantage. A definition emphasizing the construction of general theories from observation would appear to make the verbal-descriptive approach more scientific, although this activity occurs in all approaches. If scientific means precise measurement, individual differences must be considered the most scientific. Most psychologists (Cronbach, 1957; Eysenck, 1982) consider the experimental and individual differences approaches as the two disciplines of scientific psychology.

The three approaches are not completely independent. They influence each other greatly. The verbal-descriptive theories have provided ideas to test for both experimental and differential psychologists. Information discovered by experimental and differential psychologists has in turn been incorporated into revisions of the verbal-descriptive theories. Experimentalists regularly control for differential variables while differential psychologists are concerned with the effects of (experimental) treatments on prediction from individual differences. Both groups are becoming more interested in interactions between individual differences and treatments which are called aptitude-treatment interactions (Cronbach and Snow, 1977). The search for these interactions combines the strong points of both the experimental and differential approaches to psychology.

THE STUDY OF INDIVIDUAL DIFFERENCES

Differential psychologists are concerned with four broad issues—the causes of individual differences, the structure of (or interrelationships among) individual differences, the consequences of individual differences, and the treatment implications of individual differences. These four issues have not been equally studied. The concerns with the structure and consequences of individual differences have generated far more research for a longer period of time than have the other two issues. Questions about causes and treatment have, until recently, generated little direct research. Statements about these issues have often been inferred from research designed to investigate the structure and consequences of individual differences. The research done by experimentalists on causes and treatment has been inadequate because typically only environmental causes (which can be manipulated in the laboratory) are considered. Typically, treatment methods investigated by experimentalists have been developed with little regard for individual differences.

The causes of individual differences have generated numerous heated debates. These debates are collectively called the heredity-environment or nature-nurture question. Individual differences (and psychology generally) developed during the period when Darwin's theory of natural selection was highly influential. Psychological differences were regarded as being transmitted from one generation to the next by genetic mechanisms (that were yet to be discovered) in the same manner as physical differences such as height and eye color. Galton's (1874) pedigree of great men who came from a small group of families was consistent with this view. However, his pedigrees are also consistent with the possibility that different environmental characteristics of families produce different degrees of learning in their children. The resulting debate between environmentalists and hereditarians has continued for decades. The debate has regularly been declared resolved or irrelevant or a dead issue. Its continued survival during all this century suggests that it is *not* a dead issue. In fact, there is currently no more vigorous issue in psychology (*cf.*, Eysenck & Kamin, 1981).

Of the four issues studied by differential psychologists, the structure of individual differences has generated the largest amount of academic research. This issue is concerned with the question of what the fairly broad individual differences in behavior are. There is an infinitely large number of specific questions or situations that can be presented to people in which their behavior varies. Attempting to catalogue the individual differences in behavior for each possible situation would produce a very tedious and uninformative science. Rather than this, many attempts have been made to group questions and situations producing similar variations in behavior together. A technique that was developed to do this is called factor analysis, and most of the variables to be discussed in this book, such as spatial ability and extraversion, were identified using factor analysis.

Applied work with individual differences has mostly focused on the consequences of individual differences or using individual differences to predict important future behaviors. The first, and still the most frequent, behavior predicted is school achievement. Tests of individual differences (especially intelligence) have been constructed and revised to the point where quite accurate predictions of school achievement can be made (especially in the first few years of school). Predicting job performance in industrial settings, response to therapy in clinical settings, and marital adjustment in counseling settings are a few other examples of behaviors predicted from individual differences variables. The use of these predictions for selection, assignment, and personnel decisions has become very wide-spread during the twentieth century.

The treatment implications of individual differences have been considered in two ways. The first concerns itself with whether treatment is needed and is very similar to the prediction research discussed above. If a prediction is made that a person will show inadequate or undesirable behavior by using tests of individual differences combined with various background information and clinical judgment, appropriate treatment is recommended. For example, one may predict that a child with a low score on an intelligence test will have poor school achievement (assuming a large variety of other information has been appropriately considered). This prediction leads to recommendations for special treatment designed either to help the child raise his or her achievement or to allow the child to function as well as possible without academic skills. The second way treatment implications are considered deals with which of several possible treatments is likely to be most effective for a person with certain characteristics. For example, a child with good verbal skills would probably benefit more from a verbal explanation than a visual demonstration in school, while this might not be the case for a child with lower verbal skills. Investigation of treatment implications using this approach, called aptitude-treatment interactions, has only begun recently.

SOCIAL AND POLITICAL ISSUES IN INDIVIDUAL DIFFERENCES

Psychology, generally, is a socially sensitive field and the study of individual differences has more than its share of controversial topics. Popular articles on some topics such as race or sex differences in intelligence regularly appear in magazines and newspapers and influence the way people react to psychology. Even when these articles are essentially correct (which is not always the case), they are almost certain to annoy someone. The simple existence of a variable called intelligence is an affront to many people who see it as inconsistent with human equality. To suggest that intelligence might be hereditary offends those who would like to be able to change it (most notably teachers and political liberals). To suggest the opposite—that intelligence might be environmentally conditioned—is unthinkable to those who fear that they might be blamed for another's low scores (most notably parents and political conservatives). If we add the people who object to any concept inconsistent with completely unfettered free will, it should be possible to upset almost everybody in the space of one magazine page and have room for a small advertisement.

The social issues facing the study of individual differences can be divided into two broad groups—the political influences on the study of individual differences and the social influences of individual differences. These two are not independent of each other but are simply meant to allow us to consider the influence *on* and the influence *of* individual differences and their study with regard to the large society. Science is not conducted in a vacuum. It is a social enterprise that is influenced by the beliefs and biases of the scientists conducting it. This is certainly true of individual differences.

Political attitudes certainly influence the study of individual differences (Lewis, 1981; Jencks, et al., 1972). During politically conservative periods, particularly early in this century, the opinions of differential psychologists tended to be hereditarian. This was the case when intelligence tests were used to select which immigrants to admit into the U.S. During politically liberal periods, particularly the 1960's, the opinions of differential psychologists tended to be more environmentalistic. Since the late 1960's when heredity was widely dismissed as unimportant, there has been a gradual, if begrudging, change of opinion among psychologists. Heredity is now widely recognized to influence psychological variables, even by many who wish it were not true. Curiously, this change of opinion is not the result of overwhelming evidence collected in the last 10 years. Although there have been improvements during this time, the new evidence with regard to hereditary influence suggests about the same level of influence suggested by older data. (The contribution of heredity to each area of individual differences is discussed in the appropriate chapters of this book.) The change of opinion seems to correspond with the increasingly conservative political attitude during this period, rather than with changes in the evidence.

Political attitudes can bias the study of individual differences, as well as psychology in general, in either of two directions. Prevailing liberal attitudes emphasizing the desirability of social and economic equality seem to influence psychologists to emphasize environmental influences and to search for ways of reducing individual differences by environmental engineering. Hereditary influences are ignored or discounted since they threaten to limit progress toward equality. On the other hand, prevailing conservative attitudes seem to influence psychologists to emphasize hereditary influences. These influences may lend support to the hierarchical organization of society, although this organization is usually maintained by economic, military, and informational forces that are far stronger than the statements of differential psychologists. Environmental influences, in a conservative political climate, are usually seen as small and not worthy of substantial scientific investigation. An insecure conservative group might also view the possibility of environmental effects on individual differences as threatening to their status.

From Eysenck's (Eysenck & Wilson, 1978) theory of attitudes, the distinction between tough-minded and tender-minded attitudes may also influence the study of individual differences. People with tough-minded attitudes in either the conservative or liberal direction may try to impose their ideas vigorously and suppress the ideas of their opponents. People with tender-minded attitudes are more willing to allow opposing ideas to be considered, although not agreeing with them. Although tough-minded suppression is probably equally likely to come from either end of the political spectrum, in recent years, psychology has seen several examples of suppression by the environmentalists aimed at the hereditarians. Students have refused to allow noted hereditarians to give lectures and editors have been reluctant to publish the works of these people. No doubt, similar examples of suppression in the other direction could be found at some earlier time.

The student of individual differences must be aware of biases coming from his political and social attitudes as well as attempts by others to suppress or distort information. Even the most careful writers bias their work somewhat, although if they are attempting to be honest, the bias is unintentional. Likewise, the most careful reader reads and remembers information in a biased fashion. He or she also is more critical of information opposed to personal biases than of information consistent with these biases. A profitable exercise for the reader at this point is to consider what personal social and political attitudes are and state (to themselves) what results they want to find in the area. The reader may find that he or she hopes people are approximately equal, either with no differences in abilities and personality or possibly with weak points being counterbalanced by strong points. Instead, the reader may find that he or she hopes that people can be clearly ranked from extremely good on all characteristics to extremely bad on all characteristics. The reader may hope that what individual differences exist are the effects of heredity, or he or she may hope that they are caused by the environment. Whatever biases are uncovered, it will be useful to remember them while studying individual differences and to make some effort to retain information opposed to the biases. It is important to be just as critical with information that is consistent with one's biases as with information opposed to them.

Not only do social and political attitudes influence the study of individual differences, but information from individual differences may influence these attitudes. Findings indicating strong environmental effects lead to enthusiasm about using them. This enthusiasm is usually directed toward (liberal) efforts to give help where it is needed and thus reduce individual differences, although it is possible that a small group could attempt to reserve these effects for its own (conservative) use. On the other hand, findings indicating strong hereditary effects tend to discourage environmental changes. These effects are usually used to justify the *status quo*. Efforts to change society by selective breeding (eugenics) are generally considered objectionable.

The effects of information about individual differences on social and political attitudes makes certain findings appear dangerous to those who are strongly committed to one or another political viewpoint. In recent years, suggestions actually have been made that certain topics, most notably race differences, should not be studied because the findings might lend support to undesirable attitudes. These suggestions suppress possible findings or even worse advocate the acceptance of one of the possibilities without empirical evidence. While tolerance and opportunities for the advancement of all racial and ethnic groups are highly commendable goals, basing tolerance and opportunities on misinformation or suppressed information will breed cynicism that can undermine and eventually destroy these goals.

The fear that new findings in individual differences will undermine desirable political attitudes is reminiscent of the earlier fears that physical science and then, several hundred years later, biological science would undermine religious beliefs. The eventual acceptance that the sun rather than the earth is the center of the solar system has not substantially affected religious beliefs. Even the undeniable fact that the earth is roughly spherical rather than flat has had little if any, effect on basic religious beliefs. In fact, neither of these ideas, once vigorously suppressed by organized religion, seem substantially inconsistent with a belief in God. Similarly, the discovery of evolution, tracing man back to apelike ancestors, can probably be assimilated by most religious persons. Evolution is inconsistent only with the poetry and not the substance of creation.

Currently, the discovery of psychological differences between various groups should not undermine our determination to build a fair society. The conviction that "all men are created equal" is an admirable goal for any society, but as a statement of fact it can be disproved by observing a half dozen new-born babies. Differences in physical size, appearance, and health are immediately obvious. Later differences in social status, privileges, and opportunities arise. It would be truly remarkable if psychological differences did not occur. The fact that they do occur need not threaten social ideals.

CHAPTER 2
STATISTICS AND METHODS

It is impossible to study individual differences without some background in statistics. The purpose of this chapter is to provide a very basic introduction to the necessary statistics for those who have not had a course in statistics or for those who have forgotten this material. Parts of the chapter may be useful for those whose statistics courses have focused on techniques used in experimental psychology, such as analysis of variance, rather than on correlations which are more often used in individual differences. Persons familiar with correlation coefficients may skip this chapter.

This chapter is not an exhaustive review of statistics. Only topics that are necessary to understand the material in this book are covered. A reader with little or no background in statistics should be able to understand the material in the rest of the book after studying this chapter, particularly the section on the correlation coefficient. However, reading the original studies cited in each chapter will require far more extensive work in statistics. Books that deal with the statistical techniques more extensively are cited in the text.

THE MEAN

The most basic statistic that is widely used in individual differences is the mean. The mean is the average of a set of scores. Most readers of this book have figured averages, possibly the average of their test scores in a class, and should be familiar with them. The "mean" (M) is the "sum of" (Σ) all the "scores" (X) divided by the "number of" (N) scores, or:

$$M = \Sigma X/N$$

The mean is used to establish the central point of a characteristic from which people may differ. If the average weight of a group of students is 110 pounds, that does not mean that all the students weigh 110 pounds. Some weigh more and some less. The importance of the mean for individual differences is as a starting point for measuring differences above or below the average. (For more extensive coverage, see Hays, 1963 or Anastasi, 1976).

THE STANDARD DEVIATION

The most common measure of the amount that individuals differ on a characteristic is called the standard deviation. The standard deviation is the number of points that a "standard" (not exactly average, but close) person deviates from the mean.

To compute a standard deviation (SD), we first compute a variance (VAR) which is the average number of *squared* points that each person deviates from the mean. For example, in a group of three people with average weight of 110, the individual weights are 100, 110, and 120. They are 10 pounds below the mean (-10), at the mean (0), and 10 pounds above the mean (+10), respectively. Squaring these numbers shows that they are 100 squared pounds from the mean (-10^2), zero squared pounds from the mean (0^2), and 100 squared pounds from the mean (10^2). On the average, they are 66-2/3 squared pounds from the mean. This is their variance. The standard deviation is the square root of the variance. In this example the standard deviation is about 8.16 pounds. That means we should expect people to deviate from average in this sample by about 8 pounds. In a formula, the standard deviation is the square root ($\sqrt{}$) of the sum of (Σ) the squared deviations from the mean ($(X-M)^2$) divided by the number of scores (N), or:

$$SD = \sqrt{\Sigma\ (X-M)^2/N}$$

The standard deviation is the basic measure of the amount of individual differences on a characteristic present in a sample of people. Some characteristics show substantial variation among people, such as height and weight, and have large standard deviations. Others, such as number of fingers, show little variation among people and have standard deviations close to zero. (See Hays, 1963 or Anastasi, 1976).

THE STANDARD SCORE

It is often convenient to standardize a person's score on a characteristic. A standard score is the number of standard deviations above or below the mean for a particular score. For example, in a group of people with a mean weight of 110 pounds and a standard deviation of 10 pounds, John weighs 100 pounds. He is one standard deviation below the mean, or his standard score (z) is -1. Joe weighs 130 or two standard deviations above the mean (z = +2). A person who was exactly on the mean would have a standard score of 0. The standard score is a person's raw (or original) score (X) minus the mean (M) divided by the standard deviation (SD), or:

$$z = (X-M/SD)$$

(See Hays, 1963 or Anastasi, 1976).

THE CORRELATION COEFFICIENT (r)

The Pearson product-moment correlation coefficient is the work horse of individual differences. It is an index of the degree to which individual differences on one characteristic (height, for example) correspond to individual differences on another characteristics (weight, for example). A correlation of 1.0 indicates perfect correspondence and would mean that the two characteristics were identical. A correlation of 0.0 indicates that the two characteristics are completely unrelated. A correlation of -1.0 indicates a perfect inverse relationship—high scores on one characteristic associated with low scores on the other. Correlations such as .9 or .7 indicate high, but not perfect, relationships, while a .1 or .2 would indicate very slight relationships between two characteristics.

A simple formula for the Pearson product-moment correlation coefficient (r) is the sum of (Σ) the products of standard scores of two characteristics for the same person (z_1 and z_2) divided by the number of persons (N), or:

$$r = \Sigma \, z_1 \, z_2 / N$$

If characteristic 1 and characteristic 2 "go together" for a person they will be on the same side of the mean and will have the same signs (+ or -) for their standard scores. Since multiplying two +'s together gives a + and multiplying two -'s together also gives a plus, the product of the two standard scores that "go together" is plus. If most of the products are +, the correlation will be positive. If most of the products are - (opposite), the correlation will be negative. If there are about as many +'s as -'s, the correlation will be close to zero, indicating no systematic relationship between characteristic 1 and characteristic 2.

Although correlations are usually computed with large numbers of people (30 at least and preferably 100 or more), a simple example with four people is presented to illustrate its meaning. Consider people with the following standard scores (to simplify the computation) on height and weight:

	z_h	z_w	$z_h \, z_w$
John	+1	+1	+1
Jim	+1	+1	+1
Joe	- 1	- 1	+1
Jack	- 1	- 1	+1

John and Jim are both exactly one standard deviation above average on height as well as weight—they are relatively heavy and tall. Joe and Jack are exactly one standard deviation below average on both characteristics—light and short. It is clear that for each of the four persons height and weight "go together." Multiplying the standard scores for John gives +1, as it does for each of the others. Adding the products gives +4, and dividing this by 4 persons gives a correlation of +1. In the example, height and weight are perfectly correlated.

Let us change the numbers in the example and see what happens.

	z_h	z_w	$z_h\,z_w$	
John	+1	+1	+1	(go together)
Jim	+1	- 1	- 1	(opposite)
Joe	- 1	- 1	+1	(go together)
Jack	- 1	+1	- 1	(opposite)

Now, John and Joe remain the same, but Jim has lost weight and Jack has gained weight. For half of this sample height and weight go together, and for half they are opposite. Overall, we should conclude that there is no systematic relationship between height and weight in this sample. Adding the products shown in the table gives 0, and dividing 0 by 4 people gives a correlation of 0, indicating no relationship.

With larger numbers of subjects, it is convenient to think about correlations in graphical form. If we plot two characteristics on the horizontal and vertical axes of a graph, a straight line indicates a perfect (+1) correlation as in this figure:

Figure 2.1
Correlation of 1.0

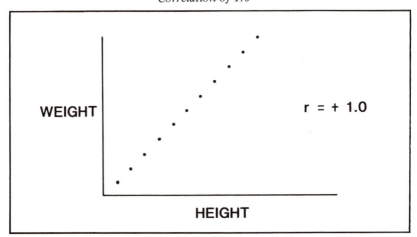

If the line tilted the other way—from upper left to lower right—the correlation would be -1. If the points are randomly scattered all over the graph, the correlation is 0. Intermediate correlations correspond to varying degrees of scatter. High correlations (+.8) have most points very close to, but not quite on, a straight line. Low correlations (+.2) have many points quite far from the straight line, but with a slight tendency to arrange themselves from lower left to upper right.

Figure 2.2
Correlation of .9

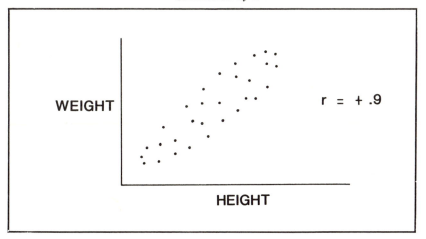

Figure 2.3
Correlation of .2

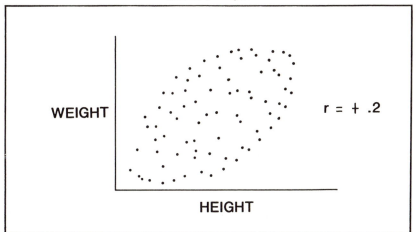

Since very few (in fact, no) psychological variables are perfectly related to each other, the degree of relationship expressed by correlations of less than +1 and greater than 0 is important. In order to get an accurate statement of the relationship between two characteristics, the correlation coefficient is squared (r^2). The squared correlation indicates the percent of variance that two characteristics share. The rest of their variance is unrelated. For example, if height and weight have a correlation (r) of .7, they would share (r^2) .49 (or 49%) of their variance with each other. The remaining 51% would be un-related, and possibly result from dieting, overeating, or genetic factors affect-ing only height or weight but not both (see Hays, 1963, or Anastasi, 1976).

NOTE ON REGRESSION ANALYSIS

Practical applications of individual differences frequently involve predicting one behavior or characteristic, such as success on a job, from other characteristics. If only one predictor is used the correlation coefficient discussed above can be used. However, usually more than one characteristic is required to give a good prediction of future behavior. Regression analysis or multiple regression allows several predictors to be combined in a single prediction equation.

As a very simple example, suppose we had three characteristics that all had correlations of 0 with each other (to simplify the example) and correlations of .7, .4, and .3 with success on a particular job. The first characteristic would predict 49% (r^2) of job success by itself, the second would predict only 16% by itself, and the third 9%. Using regression analysis, an equation could be obtained that would predict 74% of the variance of job success, leaving only 26% of its variance unaccounted for. If the predictors have correlations with each other of more than exactly 0 (which is usually the case), the problem becomes slightly more complex but still manageable with multiple regression. (See Cooley & Lohnes, 1971; or Kerlinger & Pedhazur, 1973; or Maxwell, 1977.)

NOTE ON BEHAVIOR GENETICS

Investigations of genetic determinants of behavioral characteristics depend on comparisons of correlations of the characteristics between persons who are related by varying degrees. The most common comparison involves monozygotic twins, who are genetically identical, and dizygotic twins, who share, on the average, 50 percent of their genetic material. Since both types of twins grow up in the same environment, differences in the correlations between their characteristics, physical as well as psychological, indicate the degree to which genetic factors control the characteristics. If the correlation between the heights of monozygotic twins is substantially larger than the correlation between the heights of dizygotic twins, this indicates height is genetically controlled—the larger the discrepancy between the correlations, the greater the degree of genetic influence. If the correlations are approximately equal, no genetic influence is indicated. Comparisons among related persons other than twins (siblings, first cousins, etc.) are also performed, although differences in environment (siblings living in the same home, first cousins in different homes) make these comparisons less satisfactory. Here too, higher correlations between a characteristic of highly related persons and lower correlations for less closely related persons indicate genetic influence on the characteristic. Behavior genetic analyses have been central in the most heated controversies in psychology during the last decade. (See McClearn & Defries, 1973.)

NOTE ON FACTOR ANALYSIS

Investigations of the interrelationships among individual differences variables frequently use more than the two variables which can be correlated with the Pearson formula. With large numbers of variables (items on a test, for example), the number of correlations produced by correlating each pair separately becomes unmanageable, although easily performed using a computer. To facilitate interpretation of the correlations, they are subjected to factor analysis which identifies independent factors shared by the original variables. Put in a slightly different way, factor analysis organizes the variables into groups of variables that tend to be related within the group but not related to variables in other groups. Factor analysis is useful for test construction and for identifying the important general factors in a larger domain of variables. Most cognitive abilities and personality traits have been identified using factor analysis. (See Cooley & Lohnes, 1971; or Harman, 1967; or Maxwell, 1977.)

CHAPTER 3

INTELLIGENCE

The measurement and use of intelligence tests have become highly controversial during the last decade. In 1969, Jensen published a very important paper in which he insisted that the intelligence of children limits the effects of compensatory education, that intelligence is largely hereditary, and that the racial difference in intelligence between blacks and whites is hereditary rather than a result of environmental factors. Although a large research literature on these topics existed before 1969, this paper began a popular controversy that still inspires newspaper and magazine articles more than 10 years later. During this period, numerous works have appeared (Kamin, 1974; Herrnstein, 1971; Eysenck, 1971; 1979; Jensen, 1980) that have attempted to settle or at least clarify the controversy.

During most of its history, intelligence testing has been controversial although the controversy has not appeared in the popular press as frequently as it has recently. In the late 1800's, Galton measured sensory and motor skills for the same purpose for which intelligence tests would later be used; that is, to identify those who have difficulty in learning and performing educational and occupational tasks and to identify those who are gifted in these areas. He provided suggestive, though not conclusive, evidence that intelligence (or genius in his words) is hereditary by showing that it runs in families. A cousin of Darwin, Galton was intrigued by the fact that eminent men tend to come from the same families as other eminent men. Of course, now we would not dismiss as easily as Galton the possibility that these families may provide environmental advantages to their members.

The first intelligence test appeared in 1904 when Binet (Binet & Simon, 1905) was commissioned by the French Ministry of Education to identify those children who could not profit from the regular classroom instruction provided at the time. Binet's views on intelligence were not as firmly hereditarian as were Galton's. Binet espoused what he called "mental orthopedics" for the children he identified with his test. By special training, he intended to improve the intellectual capabilities of children with low intelligence.

Binet's test contained items that were behaviorally similar to the tasks children were asked to perform in school. He asked children to count, name objects, and draw conclusions. These items might reasonably have been given by a teacher after covering the topics in class. These items differed from the sensory and motor items that Galton used in that they asked for judgment and reasoning rather than simple responses. Galton tried to analyze intellectual functioning into its component parts, while Binet tried to measure intellectual functioning at its own level in order to make practical decisions about children. Binet's effort was successful, while Galton's was not. Since that time individual differences have been almost synonymous with applied psychology.

Binet's test consisted of items that good students (nominated by their teacher) could usually answer and poor students (also nominated by their teacher) usually could not answer. Also the items on this test were those that older children answered correctly more frequently than younger children. Selecting items in this way produced a test that would distinguish good students from poor students and older children from younger children. The test measured a developmental progression as well as educational competence within each grade level.

Although the term IQ or intellectual quotient is associated with Binet (probably because of its later use on the *Stanford-Binet Intelligence Test*), this concept was actually developed by a German psychologist, Stern. Since Binet's test measured development and educational competence, the two needed to be distinguished. Now, with Binet's test there is no serious confusion between the two as long as the children being tested are the same age. If two seven-year-olds are tested, it is clear that the one with the larger number of correct items is both (a) developing mentally at a faster rate and (b) more competent in school. (Of course in practice, there are numerous exceptions due to the effects of personality, motivation, quality of teaching, family turmoil, etc.) The problem arises when children of different ages are compared, or as is more frequent, the same child's performances at different ages are compared.

Stern's solution to this problem involved correcting the score on the test for the child's age. The test score is expressed as Mental Age (MA) which is the age at which the average child answers a certain number of items correctly. In other words, if the average score of a group of children who were exactly six years old was, say, 15 points then the MA of any child (or adult for that matter) who answered 15 items correctly would be 6.0. A child's chronological age (CA) was used to correct his MA by division. The quotient, MA/CA, gives the number of MA years achieved per year of life. This quotient was multiplied by 100 so it could be interpreted as a percentage of expected development. Thus, the traditional formula for IQ is:

$$IQ = \frac{MA}{CA} \times 100$$

Let us consider some examples of the distinctions that can be made using the IQ and the MA. The first example is a simple case in which two children are the same age—for arithmetic simplicity we will use 10. If one child's test yields an MA of 10, he or she has developed mental skills at the rate of 1.0 year for every year of life (MA/CA), or an IQ of 100 (MA/CA X 100) indicates that the child has developed at 100% of the rate of the average child's development. This is an exactly average child; the average IQ at any age is 100. If the other child's test yields an MA of 12, mental skills have developed at the rate of 1.2 years for every year the child has lived. The IQ of 120 indicates that this child has developed at 120% of the rate of the average child.

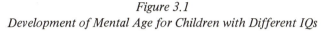

Figure 3.1
Development of Mental Age for Children with Different IQs

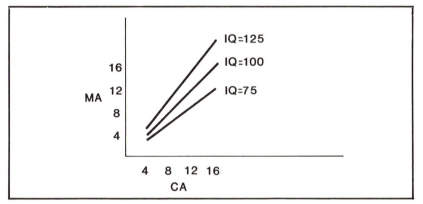

Two questions concerning these two children arise. First, which one knows more currently? This question is important for determining what to teach the children. A child should be taught information and skills (a) for which he or she has the prerequisite information and skills (i.e. subtraction before long division) and (b) that the child does not already know. The second question is, which will learn material more quickly in the near future? This question is important for determining the rate of presentation. Covering material too quickly is frustrating for the child, and covering material too slowly is boring. Both have undesirable effects on a child's academic performance.

The answers to the two questions are given by the MA and the IQ (Harter, 1965). The MA indicates the absolute knowledge of the child. In our example, the child with an MA of 12 knows more at the moment of testing than the child with an MA of 10, and the starting points for teaching these two children should ideally reflect this. The IQ indicates the rate of learning in the near future as predicted from past rate of learning. In the example, the child with 120% of average development is expected to learn more quickly than the child with 100% of average development.

In this example, it matters little whether the MA or the IQ is used for decisions. Exactly the same children will be judged to "know more" and "learn faster" using either. However, the following example illustrates the importance of the distinction. Let us compare a nine-year-old with an MA of 9 (IQ = 100) with a 15-year-old with an MA of 10 (IQ = 67). Which knows more at the moment? Clearly the child with the higher MA answered more items correctly on the test and should be given somewhat more advanced material (if academic achievement is an objective) than should the other child. Which will probably learn faster in the near future? The child with the higher IQ has learned faster in the past and can be expected to do so (in the absence of other information about the child) in the near future. In this comparison we have the first child learning faster and the second starting at a more advanced level.

What would be the likely result of simply treating both children the same? If both were taught as if they were average nine-year-olds (which is true of the first child), the end of one year's work would likely find the first child with an MA of 10 (IQ = 100) and having learned the usual year's academic material. At the same time, the second child would probably have an MA of 10.67 (unless the child has stopped advancing altogether, which is common among those with low IQs), but may have been introduced to nothing not already studied since the child started a year below MA. This treatment is clearly undesirable for the second child.

Alternatively, both could be started at material appropriate for an MA of 10 and taught at two-thirds the usual rate, which is a program that might be designed for the second child. The first child would not understand much of the new material at the beginning and would very likely give up in frustration. If the first child stayed in this program for several years and eventually caught up, that child would likely become bored by the slow pace very shortly after catching up.

Exactly these inconsistencies occur when a child is simply retained or advanced a year in school. The slower developing child who is retained is likely to be surpassed by new classmates and considered for still another retention. The faster developing child may be advanced without being taught the material in the "skipped" year.

Currently, Stern's formula for IQ is not actually used. The major tests of intelligence use the *deviation IQ*. The deviation IQ has a mean of 100 which is the same as it was with the formula and a constant standard deviation (either 15 or 16 points depending on the test) for all ages. The deviation IQ is an improvement over the IQ formula for two reasons. First, the constant standard deviation makes IQs somewhat more stable during childhood. When the standard deviations of IQs were allowed to vary, a child whose relative position in the distribution of scores was constant would have higher or lower IQs from year to year as an artifact of the distribution of scores. The gains or losses in points might erroneously be interpreted as real improvements or decrements in performance. The deviation IQ avoids this problem.

Second, the deviation IQ allows IQs to be stated for adults. The MA tends to reach a plateau late in the developmental period (roughly age 16). If this fairly constant MA in adulthood is divided by an increasing CA, the IQs would artifactually become lower and lower. With a constant mean and standard deviation, meaningful IQs can be assigned to adults. For adults, IQs are interpreted as simply a certain number of points above or below the average of 100 rather than as a percentage of average development. For children, the percentage of average development interpretation of IQ is still approximately correct and very useful.

MEASUREMENT OF INTELLIGENCE

The two most widely used measures of intelligence are the Stanford-Binet (Terman & Merrill, 1960) and the Wechsler series consisting of the *Wechsler Adult Intelligence Scale-Revised* (WAIS-R) (Wechsler, 1980), the *Wechsler Intelligence Scale for Children-Revised* (WISC-R) (Wechsler, 1979), and the *Wechsler Preschool and Primary Scale of Intelligence* (WPPSI) (Wechsler, 1967). The older of the two is the Stanford-Binet which is a revision and adaptation of Binet's original scale. This test is used from age two through adulthood and yields one IQ score, although systems to break the score into parts are often used (Meeker, 1969; Sattler, 1974). The current version of the Stanford-Binet uses the deviation IQ. The test is highly reliable with test-retest and internal reliabilities in the high .90s. This test is central in the literature of intelligence. Most of the early research (Terman, et al., 1925) was carried out with this test and, although declining in importance as the Wechsler series becomes more widely used, it is employed in much of the recent research. Virtually all new tests of intelligence are correlated with the Stanford-Binet.

Either the WPPSI, the WISC-R, or the WAIS-R can be used to test persons from age four through adulthood. These tests provide a Full Scale IQ comparable to the Stanford-Binet IQ as well as a Verbal IQ, a Performance IQ, and scores on up to 12 specific subtests. The verbal subtests on the WISC-R (there are a few differences in the names of the subtests on the three Wechsler tests) are: Information Comprehension, Similarities, Arithmetic, Vocabulary, and Digit Span. The performance subtests are: Picture Completion, Picture Arrangement, Block Design, Object Assembly, Coding and Mazes. The reliabilities of the Full Scale IQ are in the high .90s. Those for the Verbal and Performance IQs are in the low .90s, and those for the subtests are typically about .80 although they vary considerably. These additional scores make the Wechsler series more attractive than the Stanford-Binet to clinical and school psychologists and potentially more useful when the interrelationships and lower reliabilities of the subtests relative to that of the full scale IQ are considered (Kaufman, 1979). For the opposite opinion, see Brody and Brody (1976).

The Stanford-Binet IQ and the Wechsler series IQs are highly correlated with .80 being a typical correlation between the two. In general, there are a variety of intelligence tests that intercorrelate at about the .80 level. Among these are the Shipley-Hartford (Wiens & Banaka, 1960), the Otis (Cowden, Peterson & Pacht, 1971), and the Raven Progressive Matrices (Hall, 1957). Although not used clinically, a series of intelligence tests that can be self-administered is included in Eysenck (1962).

The stability of intelligence tests over long periods of time has been widely discussed (Brody & Brody, 1976). Test-retest reliability over a 12 year span from age six to age 18 (12 years) is .77. (Matarazzo (1972) reports comparable reliabilities for adults.) Another way of presenting the same data is to point out that the average child changes his IQ by about 11 points (about 2/3 of a standard deviation) either up or down during the school years. Perhaps it is easy to see how this information can be controversial. By considering these reliability figures and comparing them with the reliabilities of other psychological variables, one may easily become impressed at the relative stability of IQ. Many researchers would be happy enough to report the .77 reliability for their variables over the few weeks or months that their projects lasted. This reliability over 12 years of development from the start of school to late adolescence, compared to other psychological variables, is extremely high. In fact, IQ is without question the most stable variable over long periods of time that psychology has produced. Interestingly, many critics of intelligence present the reliability figures of their own variables as percentage agreement scores and contrast these with IQ reliabilities presented as correlations. It has recently been shown (Lewin & Wakefield, 1979; Wakefield, 1980) that percentage agreement systematically produces higher numbers than do correlations.

On the other hand, it is easy to criticize IQ because it is not perfectly stable. As mentioned above, IQs do change somewhat, especially between tests given at widely separated points in time. This criticism is not prevalent for other psychological variables. They are generally expected to be less than completely stable and are often considered useful, or at least interesting, when they can be shown to be less than completely random. That the public and even professional psychologists can be so readily shocked by clear evidence that IQ is not perfectly stable may almost be considered backhanded praise. Evidence of this sort for any other psychological variable would be met with overwhelming apathy by psychologists and the public alike.

DISTRIBUTION OF INTELLIGENCE SCORES

Intelligence tests produce distributions of scores that are approximately, but not exactly, normally distributed. By tradition the mean score is set at 100 and the standard deviation at 15 (Wechsler) or 16 (Stanford-Binet) points. Although a normal distribution theoretically extends infinitely far in either direction, almost all intelligence scores are within four standard deviations of the mean, that is between about 40 and 160. IQs above 160 or below 40 are extremely rare. Unfortunately, the low scores are not as rare as the high ones, because severe accidents and diseases can result in brain damage and IQs below 40, while no such occurrence produces exceedingly high IQs. Also, although these high and low scores are rare, they have attracted a great deal of attention due to, on the one side, their need for institutional care or, on the other, their potential value to society.

Although intelligence scores are continuous with very small, indescriminable (without a test) differences between adjacent scores, say between 119 and 120, the scores are usually grouped into verbal classifications to improve communication (Matarazzo, 1972). It must be emphasized that there are no sudden jumps between people scoring relatively high in one classification and those scoring relatively low in the next higher classification. The usual classification of IQs involves seven levels. For the lowest group with (Wechsler) IQs below 70, the term retarded is used. The development and learning of these people, compared with people scoring at higher levels, is slowed or retarded. A little over two percent of the population scores in this range. Since there are substantial differences between a person scoring 69, who can learn some elementary academic skills, and a person who cannot respond to the test at all, the American Association on Mental Deficiency (AAMD) further subdivides the retarded into four groups: mild (55-69), moderate (40-54), severe (23-39) and profound (below 25).

Figure 3.2
Theoretical Normal Distribution of Intelligence

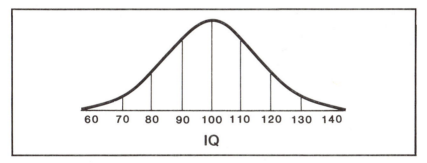

The second level with IQs in the 70s is called borderline and includes almost seven percent of the population. This group is also slow although their adjustment is better than that of the retarded. Depending on economic conditions and willingness of government agencies and families to provide services, these people may or may not be considered handicapped; thus the term borderline.

People with IQs in the 80s are referred to as dull-normal. About 16 percent of the population scores in this range. These people usually do not perform well in school but often adjust acceptably to adult life after leaving school. They are unlikely to receive special services from schools since classes for the retarded are reserved for those scoring lower and classes for the specifically learning disabled are reserved for those who score higher (usually 90 or above) and have specific learning problems rather than generally low intelligence. A frustrated teacher once referred to these children as the "shady-eighties" but dull-normal is the accepted term.

Normally "average" people have IQs between 90 and 109. Exactly 50 percent of the population have scores in this range. Above them, bright-normal refers to the 16 percent scoring between 110 and 119, and superior to the almost seven percent scoring in the 120s.

The highest classification is called simply very superior. A little more than two percent of the population score 130 or above. Most programs for gifted children include this group, although the criterion for special services for the gifted may be higher or lower from place to place. In fact in Terman's 50-year study of gifted persons, an IQ (Stanford-Binet) of 140 was used to define giftedness (Terman et al., 1925; Terman & Oden, 1947; 1959; Oden, 1968).

Of course, these classifications are made simply to aid communication. There is no more difference between a person with an IQ of 129 (superior) and one with an IQ of 130 (very superior) than there is between one with an IQ of 130 and one with 131 (both very superior), but in fact, since the tests have standard errors of measurement of from three to five points, a person who is near the boundary between two classifications is likely to be in one at one testing and the other at another testing. When IQ scores are rigidly used as cutoffs for services (this happens most frequently with scores of 70 and 130, for retardation and giftedness respectively), it is easy to forget that these numbers are simply convenient cutoffs for decisions. Too often these numbers are treated as if they represented sudden qualitative jumps in performance from retarded to normal or from gifted to *only* normal. They do not indicate sudden jumps. The difference between an IQ of 129 and an IQ of 130 is in any case trivial, and very likely simply the result of test error.

If a one point difference is so trivial, how big a difference in IQ is necessary before it is important? Due to error, even a well-trained tester with a well-constructed test cannot make discriminations of less than about three points with any confidence. (At least very little confidence should be placed in such differences.) Above three points or so, most IQ tests make fairly accurate discriminations. Without a test, we can probably distinguish between persons who differ by about 10 points after reasonable exposure to them. Differences of about 20 points are fairly easy to distinguish without a test, although differences in personality, appearance, and other variables will lead to occasional mistakes.

While deciding which person is higher or lower in IQ can be done without a test if the difference is large enough, assigning an IQ number to each person without a test would be a little more difficult. If we wanted to do this, a reasonable strategy might be to decide whether the person in question was above or below average and how far. The difficulty with this strategy is that our concepts of "average" intelligence vary considerably. People interact with and even marry people who are similar to themselves in IQ (Jensen, 1977). Thus, any person's idea of average is likely to come from those people with whom he has interacted, who will predictably deviate from average in the same direction he does. A person who has a high IQ will, then, tend to rate "average" as higher than it is and assign IQ scores that are too low to persons he or she is trying to assess. A person with a low IQ might do the opposite.

As guideposts to what various IQs mean it is convenient to discuss educational levels, since these are highly correlated (.70) with IQ and usually known (approximately) for most people with whom we are acquainted. According to Matarazzo (1972), people with IQs (WAIS) of 75 have about a fifty-fifty chance of reaching the ninth grade, although certainly not of doing average ninth grade academic work. The population average is 100, although this will have no direct meaning unless the reader happens to be average (which is unlikely, but not impossible, since he or she is studying this college text). The average high school graduate has an IQ of about 105. The average college graduate has a score of 115. The average IQ of persons receiving PhD, M.D., or similar professional degrees is about 125 (Matarazzo, 1972), although some sources (Eysenck, 1979) give somewhat higher averages.

Assuming that most readers of this book are upper level undergraduates or college graduates, the IQ of 115 is particularly relevant. These readers interact on a day to day basis with people who have an average IQ of about 115. A person they might consider below average from their experience could very well be above average compared to the entire population. The extensive norms accompanying intelligence, as well as other, tests keep us from being mislead by our biased daily experience.

CAUSES OF INTELLIGENCE: HEREDITY AND ENVIRONMENT

What causes some people to be intellectually capable and some to be severely incompetent? This question has been considered since well before Binet constructed the first practical intelligence test. The answer to the question came in three basic variations. The first answer is that intelligence is largely hereditary. The second is that it is largely environmental or a result of the person's experiences. The most recent answer is that intelligence is the result of interactions between hereditary and environmental factors.

The answer chosen by particular researchers seems to be influenced by political and social concerns, as well as by the data available to them. During the twentieth century the literature on intelligence has alternated between being mostly hereditarian and mostly environmental. Although new information has gradually accumulated that sheds new light on intelligence, the data have never changed drastically enough to account for this alteration in opinion. The political climate in which the research has been done has changed, and it has changed roughly in correspondence with changing views on intelligence.

The first, or classical, approach to intelligence is the hereditary approach. At the beginning of this century, Darwin's discovery of evolution, which described species as originating and being maintained by the genetic transmission of characteristics and the selection of these characteristics for their survival value, was a central topic of intellectual discussion. It organized biology, influenced social thought through social Darwinism, and was attacked by the church. Its importance was indisputable. Darwin's ideas very directly shaped thinking about intelligence. Not only physical characteristics, such as body size or number of teeth, are important for survival but also behavioral characteristics—alertness, reaction time, caution, and even intelligence—clearly influence survival. In this atmosphere, intelligence was thought to be a genetically determined trait that simply required accurate measurement. If environmental influences had been shown, they would have suggested that the measurement was faulty and was influenced by something other than native intelligence. Although the primary influence on the hereditarian view of the early intelligence researchers was evolutionary thought and its social application, there was some actual evidence available even then that suggested that intelligence was hereditary. It was clear then from Galton's work that intellectual competence runs in families. Now we think this observation (which is still the case) could result either from genetic or environmental similarities within families, or from both. At the time, Galton's observations seemed to be stronger evidence for genetic determination of intelligence than they would seem now.

Since then, a large amount of research has been conducted on the question of hereditary similarities in intelligence. A review of kinship correlations by Erlenmeyer-Kimling and Jarvik (1963) is particularly useful. These researchers reviewed kinship correlations reported in a large number of studies and computed median correlations for the intelligence of persons related in different degrees. Unrelated persons, who would be expected (genetically) to have a correlation of .0 between their IQs, had that correlation (actually -.10) when reared apart, but had a correlation of .24 when reared together or .20 when one reared the other (foster parent-child). The correlation increased with greater genetic similarity: second cousins, .16; first cousins, .26; uncle or aunt with child, .34; grandparent with child, .27; and parent with child, .50. For siblings and twins, finer categories were presented: siblings reared apart, .47; and together, .55; dizygotic twins of the same sex, .56; and different sex, .49; and monozygotic twins reared apart, .75; and together, .87. In general, the increasing correlations with increasing genetic similarity are supportive of genetic influence on IQ, while the differences between the siblings and twins raised apart versus together suggest a smaller environmental influence on IQ.

Recently, the technique of heritability analysis used by biologists concerned with animal breeding has been applied to intelligence data. Various analyses indicate that somewhere between 45 percent (Jencks et al., 1972) and 80 percent (Jensen, 1969) of the variation in intelligence is accounted for by heredity. Most recent investigations converge on a figure between about 60 percent and 70 percent hereditary variance (Vernon, 1979). From the empirical results, more than half of intelligence variance is hereditary and the smaller part of the variance consists of environmental effects, inter-actions, and, of course, measurement error.

The hereditarian position has not been left unchallenged. The reactions to Jensen's (1969) article were immediate and emotional. Kamin (1974) criticized the previous research in considerable detail and pointed out several shortcomings. Particularly, he exposed Burt's supposedly replicated correla-tion on monozygotic twins reared apart as suspicious. These data have since been further discredited (Hearnshaw, 1979). However, the correlation in question is available from other presumably honest sources. Nevertheless, Kamin concluded that there was no evidence that suggests the heritability of IQ is greater than 0 percent. Kamin has since been criticized severely (Eysenck, 1979) leaving his critique of heritability research less damaging.

Even if Kamin's book is taken at face value, it merely points to a relative lack of unflawed evidence for genetic influence rather than showing evidence for a lack of genetic influence. This brings us to the second answer to the question about the cause of intelligence—that is, environment. According to this view, people are born with more or less equal intellectual potential and as a result of learning experiences provided by their social and physical en-vironments become either capable or incapable. As with the early heredi-tarians, proponents of the environmental point of view are heavily influ-enced by social and political thought. In reaction to Hitler's genetically rationalized atrocities, many psychologists (along with other people) have determined to deny the existence of inherent differences that might be used to justify similar future atrocities. Unfortunately perhaps, the question of the existence of inherent differences and the question of what uses we are to make of these differences are separate. We may very well discover large inherent differences without (it is hoped) implementing a "final solution." The reaction of these people to heritable differences in intelligence is remi-niscent of the well-known reaction of a clergyman's wife to Darwin's original statement of evolution: "Let us hope it is not true; and if it is, let us hope it does not become widely known."

What evidence is there that environment affects intelligence? Skodak and Skeels (1945, 1949) showed that infants raised in adequate homes achieved IQs that were higher than would be expected if they had been raised in inade-quate homes by their biological mothers. This study has often been used to support both environmental positions and hereditarian positions since despite the evidence for an environmental effect, the correlation between biological mothers' IQs and their children's IQs (.40) was substantially higher than that between the adoptive mothers' IQs and their children's IQs (.20). The same study seems to reveal environmental and hereditary effects.

Deprivation is often cited as a reason for lowered intellectual performance by children. IQ and socioeconomic status (SES) do correlate, and this fact has been used to suggest that deprivation associated with poor living arrangements lowers IQ. However the effect could be exactly the opposite with lowered IQ resulting in poor living conditions. In fact, the available correlations suggest that this is the case with IQ correlating with a person's own SES at about .40 (Matarazzo, 1972) and with the SES of the home in which he was raised at only .19 (Glass, 1976). Eysenck (1973) has pointed out that severe sensory deprivation as used in animal experiments is very different from the economic deprivation associated with low SES and should not be expected to have the same results. Even in cases where unfortunate children have been raised in isolation, their intellectual abilities often recover dramatically following remedial efforts (Vernon, 1979).

The possible effects of nutrition on intellectual development have been widely discussed as causes of low IQ and poor school achievement. School lunch programs have been implemented in order to prevent or reverse the effects of malnutrition on intellectual development. At least one large study (Loehlin, et al., 1975) failed to find effects for severe malnutrition on intellectual development. Comparing children who were severely undernourished during their first years of life during World War II with comparable children who were adequately nourished, they found that the two groups did not differ in adulthood on intelligence, school achievement, or occupational success. The undernourished group, however, did have more physical health problems and were shorter and lighter than the properly nourished group.

Family size and birth order are two other environmental variables that seem to affect IQ. Zajonc and Markus (1975) have presented evidence that larger families produce children with lower IQs—with families of two children producing the highest IQs—and later born children having lower IQs—with the first born of the two being the highest. They explain these results with the confluence model which considers a child's intelligence to be produced (at least in part) by the opportunity to interact with persons of higher mental ages than the child's own (usually the parents). The first child has the undivided attention of two parents, and each successive child has to share parents with the older siblings, resulting in successively lower intelligence. Of course, if the older siblings are nearing adulthood themselves, they may have a positive, rather than a negative influence on the IQ of their younger siblings. This model, however, only accounts for a small number, say four or five, IQ points.

Figure 3.3
Relationship between Birth Order and IQ for Families of Different Sizes
(from Zajonc & Markus, 1975)

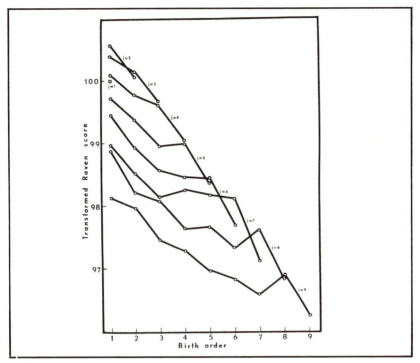

Short term efforts to improve intelligence have been widely attempted. In fact, discouragement with the effects of compensatory education was the reason Jensen (1969) raised the heredity-environment issue long after it was customary to pronounce it a dead issue. As we have seen, it is not a dead issue, but rather quite a lively one. It seems that interventions such as reinforcing correct answers with candy, practice with similar content and item format, or even reading the child the answers prior to giving the test are effective for raising scores on IQ tests by five to 10 points. However, no intervention is currently available that raises IQ over a long period of time or that has effects on the educational performance that IQ tests are designed to predict (Brody & Brody, 1976). In other words, no techniques for meaningfully changing IQ exist.

Long term changes in the natural environment may, however, affect IQ meaningfully (Brody & Brody, 1976). Although it is impossible to state exactly what change has produced the effect, the average measured IQ of the American population has risen by about a standard deviation over the last 50 years. Among the possible causes for this increase must be included longer and better schooling, better diet and health care, more urban environment, and more opportunities for work requiring higher intelligence.

The environmental explanation of intellectual differences is particularly popular in the U.S. and the U.S.S.R. (Eysenck & Wilson, 1976). It should, perhaps, not be surprising that citizens of these two "great experiments" take a jaundiced view of genetic limitations on human or societal perfectability. Environmental explanations of intellectual differences often suggest intervention techniques or social adjustments that might help these societies reach their goals. Genetic explanations, on the other hand, tend to bring the goals themselves—particularly the goal of absolute equality of both opportunity and result—into question. Historically, the Russians have fallen victim to this preference in explanation by allowing Lysenko to pursue a disastrous anti-genetic approach to agricultural products. Americans, while comfortable with the importance of genetics in farm animals and food grains, can very easily be persuaded that humans have no important genetic differences.

An important environmental characteristic to consider along with intelligence is education. Although the early intelligence tests were constructed to predict school achievement, it is quite reasonable to suspect that schooling (or lack of it) effects intelligence, which in turn predicts later educational success (or lack of it). An uncritical look at schools usually appears to justify this suspicion. It is easy to find schools (often in wealthy neighborhoods or expensive private schools) that have average student achievement levels (and average IQs) far in advance of most schools. It is very easy to conclude that some special factor about these schools—teachers, class sizes, discipline, etc.—produces the elevated performance. This conclusion is an especially easy one for the school's administrators recruiting new students and for parents seeking an effective way of advancing their children to make. It is just as easy to find schools (often in poorer areas) that have scandalously low achievement and IQ scores on the average. Once again it would appear that these schools and their teachers are not doing something right.

In order to evaluate this common observation, it is necessary to consider the initial ability levels of the students attending the schools. Parents with more economic resources tend to use these resources to enroll their children in better schools, either by buying a house close to a public school with a good reputation or by paying the tuition for a private school. In the case of the private schools, the schools select the initially better prospects and reject the others, insuring that the good reputation of the school will be maintained. At the other end of the spectrum, schools in poor neighborhoods are attended primarily by the children of parents who are unable (or unmotivated) to send them to better schools. The result is that many of the differences between schools may not be attributable to any characteristic of the schools or their teachers except for the initial differences between their students.

Careful comparisons (Mosteller & Moynihan, 1972) of schools that consider initial differences among students indicate that differences between schools have negligible effects. While school A may contain mostly highly intelligent students and school B mostly average students, any highly intelligent student would do about equally superior work whether attending school A or school B. Likewise, an average student would probably do work of similar quality whether attending school B or school A (assuming that he or she could be admitted in the first place).

Similarly, many specific characteristics of schools, such as class size, library facilities, or differences in methods of instruction, appear to have negligible overall effects on students' performance (Vernon, 1979). Of course, these variables may be effective for specific students whose learning styles or personality allow better performance in one school than another (Eysenck, 1973), but overall these cannot be said to be more or less effective schools. In fact we are as likely to find that the less attractive school is more effective for any particular student as vice-versa.

Another way of looking at the effects of education on IQ is to consider the length of schooling or whether it is available at all. This variable, in contrast to differences among schools, seems to have an effect on the development of IQ. Vernon (1979) reports studies indicating that a year of schooling has an effect of between 2½ and 5 IQ points when initial differences are considered. The unavailability of schools whether due to social circumstances (Weil, 1958), war (De Groot, 1951), or merely summer vacation (Jencks, et al., 1972) is associated with large decrements in IQ.

Another method of considering the causes of intelligence is referred to as the interactional approach or interactionism (e.g. Hunt, 1961). According to this view, considering hereditary or environmental causes of intelligence independently is a mistake—the person's genes and the environment interact to produce measured intelligence. To a certain extent this view is necessarily correct. It makes no sense to think about what a person's intelligence would be in the absence of either heredity or environment. Without genes, the person would not even exist, and without an environment, there would be no place in which to exist. Without genes or environment that are within roughly the range that commonly occur for humans, survival would be very difficult and the development of more than a minimal level of intelligence would be extremely unlikely.

For this reason, interactionist theory has been a very appealing answer to the heredity-environment question. It has suggested to a large number of textbook writers that the answer to this question is that there really is no question. However, given at least moderately acceptable genes and moderately acceptable environment, there is still the question of how they contribute to intelligence. At least two broad possibilities exist.

First, there is the possibility that heredity and environment "interact" in the statistical sense so that different people develop high and low intelligence in different environments. For example, person A might be gifted in environment X and retarded in environment Y while person B would be retarded in X and gifted in Y. If this were the case, we could simply find the right environment (note, this does not mean the one best environment) for each child and we would soon have all geniuses. Unfortunately, there is no evidence that heredity (at least with regard to intelligence) and environment do interact statistically. In fact, Eysenck (1979), in a review of kinship correlations of intelligence, argues that heredity and environment do not interact. If they did, we might expect a child to be at an advantage in intellectual development when he is raised by his biological parents (i.e., those who are genetically most similar to him) rather than by unrelated adoptive parents. The data indicate that children are neither at an advantage or a disadvantage with respect to the genetic similarity of their caretakers to themselves, but rather achieve higher IQs when raised by brighter parents regardless of their own heredity (that is, the IQs of their biological parents). In other words, environment and heredity affect IQ but they do not "interact" to do so.

The second possibility is that heredity and environment contribute independently to intelligence, but both must be considered in order to predict how intelligent a child will be. The concept of "reaction range" describes this possibility. According to the reaction range concept, a child inherits genes that determine a range of possible intelligence levels, and the environment determines whether that particular child is high or low in this range. For example, if two children received genes that would allow their IQs to reach a range of 120 to 140 (assuming no severe accidents or diseases), the child raised without a stimulating environment or encouragement to excel would have a score near 120 while the child in a stimulating environment would score closer to 140. Similarly, a child with genes limiting his potential to the range of 40 to 60 is likely to be retarded regardless of the environment, but an appropriate environment can stimulate higher levels of performance, but still in the retarded range, than would less appropriate environments. Although the reaction range concept is usually considered interactional, it is not interactional in the statistical sense. Genes and environment contribute to intelligence independently—genes first, then environment. This concept is consistent with Eysenck's (1979) argument mentioned above.

Figure 3.4
The Reaction Range Concept: Measured IQs for Persons with Different
Genetic Potential Exposed to Enriched, Normal and Deprived Environments

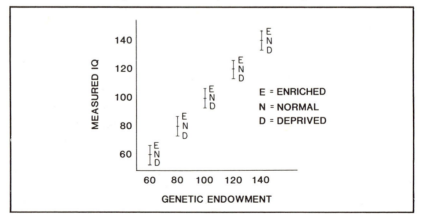

To the extent that the reaction range concept is correct, the interactional position does not resolve the heredity-environment question by denying that it is a question, but rather it simply restates it in the quantitative form in which it is usually addressed by genetical analyses. How much of IQ is genetically determined and how much is environmentally determined? If the genetic part is large, the reaction range in which a child's IQ score may vary will be small, perhaps as small as three to five points (typical standard errors of measurement for IQ tests). If the environmental part is large, the reaction range will be large, perhaps the entire range of IQ scores.

As previously mentioned, the evidence to date (Vernon, 1979) suggests that heredity accounts for 60 to 70 percent of the variance of IQ. Of course, the heritabilities that are currently available have been obtained predominantly on European or North American white samples. It is possible that the heritability of IQ would be smaller (or larger) for other groups (c.f. Scarr-Salapatek, 1971), although the size of heritabilities in other groups has not been established. Also, the heritability of IQ for whites could change if this group were subjected to different environmental conditions (and particularly different variability of environments) than is now the case. Herrnstein (1971) considers this possibility at length. He points out that if an entire population is subjected to a very narrow range of environmental possibilities, the environmental variance of IQ is necessarily low, producing a high heritability. In societies with extremely unequal distributions of wealth (and environments), the environmental variation would be larger than it is now and thus heritabilities would be lower.

CONSEQUENCES OF INTELLIGENCE

While the causes of intelligence are problematic, the consequences of intelligence are fairly clear and widely accepted. Intelligence tests were constructed to identify these consequences, particularly educational consequences, and an enormous literature using IQ to predict school success (or lack of it), occupational success (or lack of it), and social adjustment (or lack of it) has developed during the last three-quarters of a century. Although the relationships between intelligence and these practically important variables are accepted, there is controversy about the interpretation of the relationships. On one hand, if intelligence is hereditarily determined or even firmly fixed environmentally during the first five years of life, it makes sense to consider intelligence the cause of success in later life. If on the other hand intelligence only gradually develops as a result of continuing environmental experiences throughout life, it can only be considered a resultant variable rather than a causal one, and its correlations with other variables have to be explained by noting that the same influences cause both IQ and educational, occupational, and social success.

The first variable that intelligence was expected to predict was school success. Binet's task of identifying children who would not perform well in school led to the prediction of high and moderate levels of academic achievement as well as the low levels that were his main concern. The correlations of IQ with school achievement vary with different levels of schooling. The highest correlations occur in the earliest grades. In the elementary years, correlations of .70 between IQ and grades or teacher ratings are common (Brody & Brody, 1976). At the high school and college levels, correlations of about .50 are typical, and at the graduate school level these correlations drop to about .20. These correlations show that IQ is substantially related to later school achievement accounting for (by squaring the correlations) approximately 50 percent of the variance in school achievement in the early grades, about 25 percent in high school and college, and a mere four percent in graduate schools.

Two explanations for the drop in correlations between IQ and school achievement with advancing levels must be considered. Both are probably true. First, at the beginning of first grade, very few children (mostly the profoundly retarded) will not be in the class with their age mates. The differences in IQ are large, ranging from clearly gifted children to clearly retarded children. Their differences in school learning are also large and highly related to their IQs. As they advance through school, the children with the lowest IQs tend to be identified as having problems. In fairly large numbers, they are frequently either taken out of the regular class and given special training or simply drop out of school. The differences in IQ in a typical regular class become smaller each year. As the remaining children are more similar on IQ, it becomes increasingly difficult to predict differences in school achievement. By the time a particular group reaches graduate school age, all but a very narrow range of IQs (high) have been selected out of the group. The remaining small differences in IQ have a small correlation with further achievement which is itself fairly narrowly limited to high levels. If a random sample of people were enrolled in graduate school, the correlation between IQ and success would probably be very high. This reduction in correlations when the range of differences is reduced occurs with many variables (Anastasi, 1976). In general, more heterogeneous samples of people yield higher correlations.

The second explanation for the lowering of IQ-achievement correlations with advancing levels concerns the relative responsibility of the teacher and the student for learning. In the early grades, the teacher takes most of the responsibility for the child's learning. Lessons are carefully structured and supervised, and the child is continually encouraged. As the years progress, teachers leave more of the responsibility for learning to the child. Additional factors, such as motivation, importance placed on school work, and social distractions have greater influence on school learning, leaving the effect of sheer ability somewhat reduced.

The relationship between IQ and school achievement is, in general, so high that it seems worthwhile to consider whether they are simply the same variables with different names. The primary difference between intelligence and achievement tests is that intelligence items are broadly sampled to reflect ability in general while achievement items are narrowly sampled to reflect information or skills gained during a specified course of study. Of course, general intelligence is related to each achievement test, and when achievement scores are combined, they usually yield an accurate estimate of intelligence. There is some evidence that the two are distinguishable, although still highly related. Crano, Kenny and Campbell (1972) showed that intelligence predicts achievement very slightly better than achievement predicts intelligence.

Another concern about the relationship between IQ and educational achievement is whether the relationship holds for various ethnic and racial groups. The argument goes that since IQ tests sample items from white, middle class culture (and it should be noted, so does the school curriculum), the tests should not be expected to work for other groups. This concern usually goes under the name of test bias which is not very helpful because the term means too many different things. Test bias may simply refer to the fact that the mean scores of different ethnic groups are different, with about one standard deviation separating the average IQs of blacks and whites. In this sense, all intelligence tests (along with achievement tests and most ability tests) are biased in exactly the same way. Another use of the term bias is concerned with the predictive value of IQ for different groups; that is, does IQ have the same relationship to achievement for the different groups? The general answer is that the correlations are very similar for the groups that have been studied (mostly American blacks and whites), although small differences do occur (Jensen, 1979). It seems that an IQ of 85 predicts difficulty in school, a 100 predicts about average work, and a 120 predicts high quality work regardless of the ethnic background of the persons scoring at these levels.

Not only is the quality of school work as indicated by teacher's ratings or grades correlated with IQ, but the number of years a person stays in school is correlated (.70) with IQ (Matarrazo, 1972). This figure is as high as any of the correlations between IQ and grades. In fact, IQ correlations with school learning variables are pervasive. Even in programs that are specifically designed to reduce the correlations between achievement and IQ, the two variables can be shown to correlate (Vernon, 1979; Brody & Brody, 1976). Even if grades are not assigned, the time it takes a student to reach a preset learning criterion, such as the number of units mastered per unit of time or the number of repetitions necessary to reach mastery, all correlate with IQ at about the same level as do traditional teacher grades.

After the school years, IQ correlates with occupational attainment (.50) at about the same level it correlates with school grades. When occupations are ranked (from professional and managerial, through skilled and semi-skilled, to unskilled), persons in the higher levels have, on the average, a higher IQ, although there is a great deal of overlap. Although it would be highly unusual, it would be possible, if we looked long enough, to find an individual in the highest occupational group with a lower IQ than an individual in the lowest. One reason for the correlation between occupational attainment and IQ is that education limits access to the more prestigious occupations, and IQ correlates with educational success and years in school. In order to become a physician or a lawyer, a person must stay in school about 20 years. At various points in their schooling, they must pass selection tests that allow them to continue, and finally they must pass a licensing exam. All of these hurdles are correlated with IQ, making it extremely unlikely that a person with low IQ could enter these occupations. People with lower IQs can gain entry to lower level occupations without staying in school for a long period or passing numerous tests. Of course, there is nothing to keep people with higher IQs out of these jobs either. Extremely bright people, who are either unmotivated for occupational advancement or simply extremely unlucky, are occasionally found in lower level jobs (Terman & Oden, 1959). Apparently, high IQ does not insure success as effectively as low IQ bars success.

Once entrance has been gained to an occupation, IQ seems to be less important for success in it (Ghiselli, 1966). Correlations of about .20 are typically found between IQ and job performance. It may seem strange that IQ has a small correlation with how well a job is done while having a much larger one with which job a person does. It is actually not that surprising. Several reasons have been suggested for the lower correlation with job performance. First, the range of IQs in any one job is restricted, reducing the size of the correlation between IQ and any other variable, such as job success, for each group. Imagine trying to correlate IQ and the number of cases won for lawyers. Since initially all lawyers have moderately high to high IQ, the fairly low IQs that would be expected to lose all their cases are simply missing from the sample. Second, there is considerable difficulty measuring job performance. A supervisor who is asked to identify good workers and poor workers is very likely to confuse personal feelings for each employee with the actual quality of their work. This criterion problem, as it is called, lowers correlations. Third, the relationship between IQ and job performance at some jobs may be curved with workers of intermediate intelligence out-performing those at either extreme. It is easy to imagine that on some tedious jobs persons with low IQ would have difficulty mastering the work while those with average IQ would have no difficulty. For those with very high IQs, the tedium might produce low motivation or they might actively seek distraction and thus perform less well than the average person. Since correlations only reflect linear relations (that is high IQs with high performance, middle IQs with middle performance, and low IQs with low performance), the curved relationship between IQ and performance may be missed on many jobs. Probably, the linear correlation of .20 is an underestimate of the relationship between IQ and success on a job when curved relationships are included (Brody & Brody, 1976).

PRACTICAL USES OF INTELLIGENCE

Three practical applications of intelligence test data are diagnosis, selection, and assignment. They are not completely separate applications, and any intelligence test that is given is likely to be used for more than one of these purposes.

Diagnosis refers to the activity of trying to find out "what is wrong" with a person or whether there is anything at all wrong with the person. Intelligence tests are widely used for this purpose in medical and educational settings. The IQ itself is informative about the severity of a problem, particularly of retardation, and about educational and social obstacles to treating other problems—for example, bright neurotics are easier to treat than dull neurotics. As for differential diagnosis, that is distinguishing one type of problem from another, the IQ by itself is of limited value (Sattler, 1974). Not only retardation, but schizophrenia, autism, brain damage, parental neglect, conduct disorders, and senility are associated with lowered IQs. Of course, specific learning disabilities are defined as showing average or above average intelligence, and anxiety and fears are not particularly related to intelligence. In general, IQ is one important index of the severity and difficulty of treatment for all these problems. The most widely used tests, the Wechsler series, produce subtest scores that, when used along with other information, contribute more to differential diagnosis than does the overall IQ score. The overall IQ is so pervasively related to intellectual problems that its ability to distinguish among problems cannot be high. It may be considered analogous to a thermometer which can be considered roughly a measure of physical well being but must be used along with other data to contribute to differential diagnosis.

The second practical application of intelligence is selection. This application is associated with personnel departments of private industry and government agencies, as well as with admissions offices of colleges, graduate and professional schools, and exclusive private schools at lower levels. Selection basically involves using IQ (and other information) to choose the candidates who are most likely to be successful at a given activity. When intelligence tests are used to select applicants from a fairly diverse group, they can be used for selection successfully. When, however, the applicants have already been screened for ability by other tests, previous experience, or possession of educational credentials, IQ will add little useful information to the selection process. Selection is currently the object of a great deal of legal controversy. Since different ethnic groups score differently on IQ tests while yielding largely equivalent correlations between IQ and performance, the process of completely fair selection is elusive. If equal probability of success for each individual is used as the selection criterion for a position, certain groups will be underrepresented in this position, and the process is said to be unfair to these groups. If equal representation of groups is the selection criterion, less qualified (and less likely to succeed) individuals will be selected over more qualified individuals, and the process is said to be unfair to those individuals (Brody & Brody, 1976). It should be noted that stating probabilities of success is not difficult; the difficulty lies in how we use these probabilities in combination with social goals, such as the inclusion of ethnic minority groups at all professional levels.

The third use of IQ is assignment. Assignment occurs when each individual is placed in the environment that is expected to produce optimal levels of some outcome (most frequently school achievement). Assignment is appropriately used when it is based on knowledge of interactions between IQ and environmental variables, so that persons at a certain IQ level can be expected to perform best in setting A while those at another level perform best in setting B. It should be noted that for assignment to occur a person need not be physically moved. If a teacher individualizes instruction, teaching different students in appropriately different ways, assignment has occurred. Cronbach and Snow (1977) have reviewed the literature on the interaction between intelligence and instructional methods. At present, assignment on the basis of IQ should consider three characteristics of the teaching environment. Structure should be considered, with students of low and average IQs being generally provided with a high degree of structure to produce optimal achievement and those with high IQs being generally given less structure and allowed to provide their own. Speed of coverage is optimally higher for bright students and lower for duller students. Outside the optimal range for each student, frustration or boredom may undermine achievement. Depth of coverage or number of details can be greater for brighter students. Once again frustration or disinterest may occur if the level of detail is inappropriate for a student.

These applications of intelligence—diagnosis, selection, and assignment—can be used either by the person, usually with the help of a counselor, or by an institution for its own purposes. This distinction is clearest in the case of selection. A personnel officer of a company selects applicants for the benefit of the company. The welfare of the applicant is not an issue unless he or she is actually selected. A vocational counselor, on the other hand, uses data that are very similar to those used by the personnel officer, but allows the individual person to anticipate possible selections based on these data and adjust goals in accordance with them. In other words, applicants can select the most desirable situation for which they are realistically likely to be selected.

The distinction between the use of intelligence scores by a person or by an institution should be maintained for diagnostic and assignment applications as well as for the selection application discussed above. In the case of persons with low IQs being considered for various diagnostic categories, a guardian should be available to assure that the person's interests do not become confused with or disregarded in favor of institutional goals or simple convenience. Likewise, the interests of the person and the institution should be distinguished for assignment. The goals to be optimized might very well be different for the person (perhaps, taking advantage of immediately marketable vocational skills) than for the institution (perhaps increasing average reading and math achievement). Different goals usually dictate different assignments. Parents or guardians have to assert the individual's goals when these conflict with institutional goals.

SUMMARY

Individual differences in intelligence have been reviewed. Intelligence was first practically measured by Binet in 1904 to identify French school children with educational difficulties. Conceptually, though not for current test scoring, IQ is the ratio of mental age to chronological age expressed as a percentage. IQ has a mean of 100 and a standard deviation of about 15 points. It is extremely stable over long periods of time, but it is not absolutely fixed. IQ is predominantly influenced by hereditary factors (most likely 65 percent to 70 percent of its variance) but also is substantially influenced by long term environmental factors and length of education. IQ predicts a wide range of educational and occupational variables and is used for diagnoses, selection, and assignment.

CHAPTER 4

COGNITIVE ABILITIES

From the first attempts to measure intelligence, questions about the nature and structure of intellectual ability were posed. A particularly central question was whether there was one intelligence or many separate intelligences or abilities. Galton wrote about eminence or genius as if one concept was central. However, his attempts at practical measurement included a wide variety of simple sensory and motor skills, each measured separately. He assumed that if enough traits such as visual acuity or strength of grip could be measured the presence or absence of genius would be revealed. His measures only had small correlations with success at college and other practical criteria of intelligence and were never widely used in practice. (It should be noted, however, that Litner Witmer who is considered the first clinical psychologist and the first school psychologist used similar measures in his clinic.)

Binet's view of mental abilities was not too different from Galton's although it is common now to contrast Binet's general intelligence test with Galton's many tests of small skills. Binet actually discussed "intelligence in general" which allows the possibility that multiple abilities exist but suggests that his test was concerned with an overall index of abilities "in general." Binet's measurement program was also more directly concerned with a specific application than was Galton's. Since Binet had only one task—to find the children who would not profit from regular classroom instruction—it was reasonable to provide a single index (later the IQ) that would distinguish between children who would learn in school and those who would not. The items on Binet's test were more similar to school work than were Galton's tasks, and Binet simply discarded items that did not work. Apparently, Galton did not do this as he was interested in the measurement of a variety of individual differences rather than immediate application. In fact, Binet discarded some surprising items, such as those requesting creative or original responses, because they simply did not distinguish between students that teachers nominated as good students and those nominated as bad students. Since then, intelligence tests have usually not included creativity items, and when creativity is measured, it is measured separately from intelligence.

At about the same time Binet was working, Spearman (1904, 1927) distinguished between general intelligence (g) and specific skills (s). Spearman used a technique called factor analysis that he was largely responsible for developing to identify g and many s's. Factor analysis is a complex numerical technique that has been greatly refined since Spearman used it, but for our purposes it can be viewed simply as a way to summarize the information in a large number of correlation coefficients. Variables, usually test items, that are positively intercorrelated among themselves are included on one factor (and are said to "load on" that factor). Another set of items that are intercorrelated among themselves, but not correlated (or only slightly correlated) with the first set load on the second factor, and so on until all the important factors are identified.

Spearman noticed that when he intercorrelated and factor analyzed a set of ability type items (that is, items with right and wrong answers as opposed to items asking for original responses, self-descriptions or opinions), most of them were moderately highly positively correlated with each other, and these formed one general ability factor (g). There were usually several smaller or specific (s) sets of items that formed additional factors that altogether did not account for as much variance as the g factor. In fact, a typical item would load highly on (i.e., be strongly correlated with) the g factor and have small loadings on (i.e., have weak correlations with) one or more s factors. This result suggested that responses to the items were predominantly influenced by general ability while other small skills—speed, visual acuity, finger dexterity—also influenced responses to the items.

Spearman's primary concern was with finding items that loaded only on g, that is measured g without the influence of any s's. In the process, however, he also identified items that measured various skills that were distinguishable from g, and this contributed to the measurement of separate abilities. It is still common practice in the clinical or educational assessment of abilities to measure a person's intelligence (g) and to supplement that measure with whatever other abilities (s) are considered important for that particular case—such as attention, memory, eye-hand coordination, to mention only a few. In fact, one currently used test, the *General Aptitude Test Battery,* is designed to give a general ability score and scores for several specific skills in order to contribute to employment decisions.

Of course, it is possible to try to analyze g into a set of smaller s's until mental ability is viewed as a very large set of specifics which produce g only when added together. This is similar to the program Galton had pursued before Spearman and to the program Thomson (1941) pursued just after Spearman. In fact, the idea has recurred fairly frequently during this century and currently influences, though usually not explicitly, approaches such as mastery learning, task analysis, behavioral objectives, and precision teaching. All these approaches have in common a focus on the smallest possible unit of behavior. The problem with this idea is the data. It has been repeatedly found (Vernon, 1979) that the specific behaviors are generally positively correlated, so that a person who is good at one is likely to be good at most of the rest, and a person who is poor at one is likely to be poor at most of the rest. This fact makes the explanation of intelligence as a sum of separate independently acquired skills less compelling than the explanation of the learning of specific skills as a function of some general ability. The second explanation accounts for the intercorrelation of the different measures while the first seems to suggest that they should not be correlated.

Thurstone, who also contributed to the development of factor analysis, pursued a program of research that was intermediate between that of Binet (all g) and that of Thompson (many s's). He set out to summarize the field of mental abilities into a smaller number of primary mental abilities that would be more general than s's but not as inclusive as g. Using factor analysis, he identified seven primary mental abilities, that is seven sets of items that could be separated by their high correlations with other members of their own factor and lower correlations with items outside their own factor. The seven factors were called Verbal, Space, Reasoning, Number, Rote Memory, Word Fluency, and Perceptual Speed, and are still widely used in the *Primary Mental Abilities Test* and have influenced the construction of a large number of other tests. Toward the end of Thurstone's career, it was shown that these factors, although separable, were not independent and would yield a general factor when they were subjected to further factor analysis (Eysenck, 1939). Thurstone (Thurstone & Thurstone, 1941) agreed that this was correct. All widely used batteries of ability tests yield a measure that correlated highly (about .80) with general intelligence tests whether the battery is presented as a separate abilities battery (such as the *Differential Aptitudes Test* or the *Illinois Test of Psycholinguistic Abilities*) or as an intelligence test with more specific subtests (such as the Wechsler series).

Figure 4.1
Guilford's Structure of Intellect Model (from Guilford, 1979)

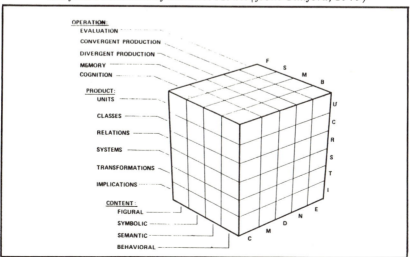

Figure 4.2
Hierarchical Model of Abilities

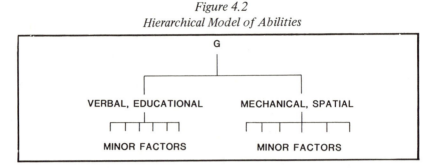

Current theories of mental abilities treat abilities as both separable—and meaningful and useful when separated—and as parts of a larger organized whole which may be referred to as intelligence, g, or intellect. Some test constructors use fairly transparent euphemisms such as scholastic aptitude, mental maturity, and general cognitive ability to sidestep the continuing controversy that has focused on the word intelligence. Guilford (1967, 1979) deals with the organization of abilities by considering the contents, products, and operations involved. Abilities that include the same contents, products, or operations are similar and can be isolated by factor analysis, while those that share no contents, products, or operations in common are dissimilar. Vernon (1961) views intelligence as hierarchically arranged with g being composed of verbal-educational factor and a spatial mechanical factor. These two factors are composed of still smaller factors all of which are positively correlated. This theory is in agreement with the structure of most practically used ability tests.

MEASUREMENT OF ABILITIES

A variety of test batteries are used to measure abilities for various settings. Different tests are used for clinical, educational, and occupational purposes. Although the tests used in the different settings have been independently constructed for their particular uses, they generally measure a fairly small number of abilities with similar subtests that correlated highly from one test battery to the other.

In clinical settings, abilities are measured by intelligence tests and by tests specifically designed to measure separate abilities. The *Wechsler Adult Intelligence Scale* (WAIS) is the most frequently used test for measuring abilities in clinical settings. Besides the IQ, the WAIS yields a general verbal ability score and a general non-verbal ability score, called Verbal IQ and Performance IQ, respectively. These scores have reliabilities in the .90s and are positively correlated with each other (about .60) while being distinguishable with factor analysis (Matarazzo, 1972). The verbal-performance distinction is related to sociopathic personality when performance is higher than verbal and treatment success when verbal is higher than performance. Deficiencies in verbal scores are used to indicate damage or malfunction in the left cerebral hemisphere which controls speech, simple logic, serial memory, and right sided sensory and motor functions for virtually all right handed persons and most left handed persons. Deficiencies in performance scores are used to indicate damage to the right hemisphere which controls spatial visualization, spatial transformations, spatial memory, and left sided sensory and motor functions for virtually all right handed and most left handed persons.

The 12 subtests give measures of moderately distinct, although positively correlated, abilities. Among the verbal subtests, vocabulary, general information, and arithmetic measure the school related abilities suggested by their names. Similarities measures a higher level logical ability involving classification of specific words. Comprehension measures verbal social skills including knowledge of values and verbal fluency. Digit span measures short-term memory for series of numbers read aloud. Among the performance subtests, block design and object assembly measure the ability to construct a visual whole, either abstract (block design) or concrete and familiar (object assembly), from its parts. Picture completion measures attention to visual detail. Picture arrangement requires the subject to recognize a short sequence of events from visual cues. Digit symbol measures eye-hand coordination as does the mazes subtest.

Some of the tests have been observed to decline with age—Digit Span, Similarities, Digit Symbol, and Block Design—and are called the "don't hold" tests, while others—Vocabulary, Information, Object Assembly, and Picture Completion seem not to decline or to decline only minimally with age and are called the "hold" tests. These two groups of tests are compared to estimate the degree of deterioration that may have occurred due to senility or to a psychotic break. The "hold" tests estimate premorbid functioning, and the "don't hold" tests estimate current functioning. This comparison must, however, be used with caution (Matarazzo, 1972).

Clinical tests other than intelligence tests used to measure abilities have mostly been designed to indicate neurological malfunctioning. The *Bender-Gestalt Test* is a test that is used to screen for general brain damage. It requires the subject to copy a series of designs with a pencil. The extensive Reitan battery consists of a large number of tasks giving more specific indications of malfunctioning. The various tasks tap visual, auditory, and motor control abilities. Patterns of failures on the tasks are used to suggest the location and extent of brain damage.

In educational and child-clinical settings, the variety of ability tests is greater than in other settings. This is the result of the longer period of time that tests have been used in these settings and the larger number of people involved in education as compared with clinical psychology or vocational guidance. As in clinical settings, intelligence tests, such as the *Wechsler Intelligence Scale for Children - Revised* (WISC-R) are used to measure specific abilities. The use of the verbal, performance, and 12 subtest scores are similar to their use on the WAIS and will not be repeated here (Glasser

& Zimmerman, 1967). In addition to these factors there has recently been much interest in a third factor, attention or freedom from distractibility, especially with children (Kaufman, 1979). This ability is measured by the digit span, coding, and arithmetic, subtests of the WISC-R.

A widely used test for children based on an extensive model of abilities is the *Illinois Test of Psycholinguistic Abilities* (ITPA) (Kirk & Kirk, 1971). The ITPA is based on a promising model of abilities (Doughtie, et al., 1974) that includes auditory and visual subtests, higher-level (representational) and lower level (automatic) subtests, as well as receptive, expressive, and organizing subtests. The test is constructed to produce lower correlations among its subtests than typically occur on intelligence tests. This characteristic makes identifying patterns of disabilities with the ITPA more reliable and useful for learning disabled children than it is with the WISC-R. Nevertheless, the subtests are still substantially related (Alston & Wakefield, 1974), the ITPA subtests are highly related to the WISC-R (Wakefield & Carlson, 1975).

Guilford's *Structure of Intellect* (SOI) theory has been widely applied to ability measurement in schools. Meeker (1969) has presented techniques for rescoring the WISC-R, ITPA, and the Stanford-Binet for the SOI factors (Meeker, Mestynek & Meeker, 1975), and has constructed a test battery specifically for measuring the SOI factors. Patterns of scores on this test are useful for predicting school achievement (Thompson, et al., 1978). The SOI model distinguishes among abilities based on the contents, or basically the information to be used, the (cognitive) operations to be applied to the information, and the product that results (Guilford, 1979). The various combinations of contents, operations, and products produce 120 small abilities, most of which have been isolated by factor analysis. Of course, measuring all 120 would be a very time consuming task. Normally only a few of them are used for practical purposes.

At higher levels, tests such as the *Scholastic Aptitude Test* (SAT) and the *Graduate Record Exam* (GRE) are used to select students for college and graduate school. Both tests have been considered intelligence tests, ability tests, or achievement tests. For selection into higher education, the distinction among these types of tests becomes blurred. For our present purposes it is reasonable to consider them to be ability tests since they produce separate verbal and quantitative scores. These scores have reliabilities above .90, are separable, yet positively correlate as do most ability scores. As with most ability tests, the verbal scores are generally more predictive of academic success than are other parts of the tests (quantitative in this case).

In occupational settings, ability tests are used for selection and for advisement. Tests used for selection are normally constructed for the company that will use the test and are carefully guarded, so an applicant will not be able to practice on the test or find out the answers in advance. Like the items, the reliabilities and validities of these tests are usually known only to company personnel unless the tests are brought under examination in legal proceedings.

The *Differential Aptitudes Test* is widely used for vocational guidance (Bennett, Seashore & Wesman, 1951) especially for high school students. It consists of eight subtests with reliabilities mostly in the high .80s and correlations among themselves generally in the .40s and .50s, except for the Clerical Speed and Accuracy subtest which has negligible correlations with the rest. The first two subtests, Verbal Reasoning and Numerical Reasoning give information about probable academic success. Mechanical reasoning, Space Relations, and Abstract Reasoning suggest success (or lack of it) at a variety of technical and mechanical jobs. Clerical Speed and Accuracy, Spelling, and Grammar give useful information about a person's probable success in secretarial, white collar, and teaching jobs.

CAUSES OF COGNITIVE ABILITIES

In considering the causes and development of cognitive abilities, several important central facts must be kept in mind. One fact is that cognitive abilities are virtually all positively correlated (e.g. Yom, Wakefield & Doughtie, 1975). For reliable tests of the different abilities, the correlations are substantial with .5 being typical. These correlations mean that, in general, a person who scores high on a test of one cognitive ability is likely to score high on tests of other cognitive abilities although there will be numerous exceptions. Similarly, a person who scores low on one ability test is likely to score low on other ability tests.

The positive relationships among ability tests are contrary to the relationships most people expect (or hope) to find among them. It is fairly common for people to react to a person who is very good at something (say mathematics) by suggesting that he or she is very bad at other things (say using tools). This reaction avoids the possibility that the person who is good at math may be generally more able than the person who is not as good at math. We seem to believe that people's strong abilities are compensated for by weak abilities so that any person who is good at one thing must be bad at another to even things out. On the other end of the spectrum, students with clearly observed weaknesses in abilities often inspire years of fruitless searches for the strong points their parents and teachers believe they must have to make up for their weaknesses. Another variation of this theme is our current effort in educational settings to specify every child's strengths and weaknesses. However, for children with school problems, these lists, rather than being appropriately balanced, are usually heavily weighted with weaknesses.

If people's abilities were compensating so that every weakness was balanced by a strength, we would not find positive correlations among the abilities. We would find negative correlations indicating that high scores on one test were associated with low scores on another. This is not true—in general or for any pair of abilities that have been investigated. Compensating abilities simply do not exist.

If abilities do not compensate for one another, perhaps they are simply unrelated. If a child cannot do math, maybe we will be able to find something else he just happens to be able to do well. Once again, the positive correlations make this unlikely. If performance in different areas were independent, we would find near zero correlations among the abilities. While a few near zero correlations are found such as between problems requiring speed and accuracy and those requiring the solution of difficult tasks without time limits, most measures of different abilities are positively correlated.

The second fact that must be considered is that virtually all ability measures are positively correlated with measures of general intelligence. This fact is not completely independent of the first. Since abilities are positively correlated among themselves, it is not surprising that they are positively correlated with tests of general intelligence that have items reflecting many specific abilities (Humphreys, 1962).

The third fact is that the correlations are not uniform. Ability tests have repeatedly been found to group together (using factor analysis) into a small number of still positively correlated general abilities (Vernon, 1961). In other words any ability test is likely to be positively correlated with any other ability test, but its correlations with some tests are higher than its correlations with other tests.

Several sets of ability factors have been suggested. Thurstone suggested seven primary mental ability factors, and Guilford suggested an array of 120 factors. The most widely discussed organization of abilities, however, consists of two factors. Vernon (1961) called these very broad factors verbal-educational and spatial-mechanical and broke each of these into more specific factors. It is also common to consider these (or similar) factors to be simply visual and auditory factors (Paivio, 1971; Delaney, 1978). This distinction is very popular with school psychologists and teachers since it suggests that visual and auditory learners can be presented information either visually or auditorially to improve their performance. A similar distinction has recently been made between simultaneous processing ability and successive processing ability (Das, Kirby & Jarmin, 1975). Simultaneous processing involves spatial visualization and can be considered roughly equivalent to the visual factor mentioned above, while successive processing involves working with sequences of items and is similar to, but not completely limited to, auditory abilities (Kirby & Das, 1978).

This distortion between auditory and verbal abilities, or successive and simultaneous abilities, or verbal and spatial abilities has often been related to the different functions of the left and right cortical hemispheres (Sperry, 1968; Naylor, 1980). The left hemisphere is associated with the verbal, auditory, or successive factor, while the right is associated with the visual, spatial, or simultaneous factor. An alternative conceptualization based on the Russian psychologist Luria's work has the forward areas of the brain controlling the successive processing and the rear areas controlling the simultaneous processing (Das, Kirby & Jarmin, 1975). This view strengthens the connections between visual and simultaneous processing and auditory and successive processing, since the same two areas of the brain control visual (rear) and auditory (front) processing as are held to control simultaneous and successive processing, respectively.

What general causes of cognitive abilities might result in abilities that are positively intercorrelated and correlated with general intelligence while showing some patterns in their intercorrelations? The answer to this question is limited by the answer to questions about the causes of general intelligence. Since cognitive abilities are subfactors of intelligence, the causes of intelli gence and the causes of abilities must be the same. If intelligence is said to cause abilities, then whatever causes intelligence must in turn be the cause of abilities, and vice-versa. Since the data for intelligence indicate a predomi- nance of genetic causation, and since there is evidence of the genetic causa- tion of several separately measured abilities (DeFries, Vandenburg & Mc- Clearn, 1976; McGee, 1979; DeFries et al., 1976), then genetic factors must be considered prime candidates as causes of abilities.

To be consistent with the observed correlations among ability variables, genetic causes would have to work in a hierarchical fashion. Some genes must result in general intellectual ability, and other genes must affect more specific abilities within the limits set by the general genes. The general effects come from a large variety of genes that influence general health and development, blood flow to the brain, and the electrical and chemical properties of the brain (cf., Hendrickson & Hendrickson, 1980) to mention only a few. Genes resulting in advantageous general characteristics would tend to raise all abili- ties, while those that result in disadvantageous general characteristics would lower all abilities. More specific genes might favor the right or left side of the brain or favor either the auditory or visual neural structures. The addition of these genes to the general ones would result in some differences among the abilities of the same person while leaving all abilities within a somewhat restricted range. Genes acting in this fashion would result in abilities that are distinguishable, yet positively correlated. This has been known to be their organization for several decades (Eysenck, 1939).

Physiologically, the organization of general intelligence into two posi- tively correlated factors with even smaller subfactors seems reasonable. The nervous system is, of course, one system with massive and redundant inter- connections among its parts. Even when connections are severed intention- ally, other connections allow the system to work in a unified fashion, except when situations are very carefully contrived to present information to only one part of the system such as is done in split-brain research (Sperry, 1968). That all cognitive abilities are part of the "g" (general intelligence) factor is consistent with the redundant interconnection and interdependence of dif- ferent areas of the brain. At the next level, the eyes, optical nerves and occipital lobes serve visual processing with the right hemisphere generally being involved in visualization and manipulation (McGee, 1979). That a visual-spatial factor (and several subfactors) should emerge from ability tests reflects the efficiency of this extended physiological visual system relative to other cognitive systems. In addition, the auditory system includes the ears, connective nerves, and temporal lobes, and is supplemented by the left hemisphere for language tasks. An auditory factor (and subfactors) is also evident in cognitive ability tests.

An environmental explanation for the observed organization of abilities is possible but must take a certain form. An explanation that involved only simple, passive reception of environmental stimuli would not reflect the actual organization of abilities. If a group of people who were all cognitively identical at birth were exposed to varying stimuli for varying lengths of time, the expected result would be negative correlations among abilities since time spent with one stimulus would be time *not* spent with another. A more complex environmental explanation must be considered. Such an explanation would have to suggest a variable (or several) that would structure the abilities in the correct manner. One possible variable is the mediation of stimuli by auditory and visual systems. Using this variable, the environmental explanation is very similar to the physiological one presented above.

Another possibility is that one environment might be generally more or less conducive to cognitive development than others, and that smaller cultural variations might favor the development of some abilities over others. Lesser, Fifer and Clark (1965) have presented some data along these lines. Socioeconomic status was related to general ability level, while ethnic group (culture) was related to differences in ability patterns. Using Thurstone's *Primary Mental Abilities Test,* these researchers found that black children had relatively high verbal scores and lower numerical and spatial scores. Although the scores of Jewish children were uniformly higher than the blacks, they had a similar profile of higher verbal and lower spatial scores. Puerto Rican children had lower verbal and higher spatial and numerical scores. Similar to the Puerto Rican children but at a higher overall level, Chinese children had a lower verbal and higher spatial, numerical, and reasoning profile. For all four ethnic groups, the profiles of lower and higher social class subgroups had similar patterns, with the higher social class group having all scores elevated above those of the lower social class group. Although the explanation of cultural causes of ability patterns may account for some observed group differences, if it accounted for most individual differences, we would expect to see qualitatively different cognitive factors in the different ethnic groups. In fact, the same factors appear in all the groups that have been studied (Kaufman, 1979).

Short-term treatments to improve specific cognitive abilities have been widely applied. The rationale for these treatments is, in brief, that if a child does poor work because of a weakness in auditory abilities, for example, improvement of the auditory abilities should result in generally improved school work (Kirk & Kirk, 1971). Unfortunately such attempts to improve children's performance by treating their cognitive abilities have generally not been as successful as expected. Just as in the case of general intelligence, scores on specific ability tests can be raised by small amounts with careful training. However, the everyday school performance to which these abilities are related does not usually improve along with the ability test scores. Meaningful change in cognitive abilities has, thus far, been elusive.

CONSEQUENCES OF COGNITIVE ABILITIES

Just as with the causes of cognitive abilities, their consequences must be considered with their intercorrelations in mind. Since most cognitive abilities are positively intercorrelated and positively correlate with intelligence, we might expect that most abilities correlated positively with the criteria that intelligence tests predict. This is, in fact, what is generally found.

It is not, however, what is generally expected of or hoped for ability tests. Once again, the idea of compensating abilities makes many people expect that even a person with the lowest overall performance on ability tests will have one strong ability and consequently one occupation or educational option in which he will excell. In general, this does not happen, although anecdotes about *idiots savants,* who are extremely retarded yet have one well-developed ability, are discussed by psychologists far in excess of their very small numbers and their importance to psychology. Even among psychologists, any slight indication of compensating abilities is eagerly received while the massive amount of evidence suggesting that abilities are positively correlated is viewed as somewhat disappointing.

There are some distinctions among ability tests that result in differences in the size of correlations between the tests and the educational or occupational criterion (Ghiselli, 1966). These different sized correlations indicate tests that are differently related to the criteria. An important distinction is between verbal ability tests and non-verbal ability tests. Verbal tests, such as the Verbal IQ of the Wechsler tests, Verbal Reasoning on the *Differential Aptitude Test,* and the verbal scores on the *Scholastic Aptitude Test,* correlated with most academic criteria higher than do the equally well constructed nonverbal parts of the same tests. For example, the Verbal IQ on the Wechsler scales correlates with overall grades about as well as the Full Scale IQ does (.50 to .70), while the Performance (nonverbal) IQ has correlations of only .20 with grades. This difference holds for all the ethnic groups that have been considered (Kaufman, 1979). Similarly, the Verbal Reasoning subtest of the *Differential Aptitude Test* and the verbal score on the *Scholastic Aptitude Test* give moderately high correlations with college grades (.50) while other subtests on these tests give far lower correlations. On the other hand, the math test on the *Scholastic Aptitude Test* predicts *choice* of college major better than does the verbal test (Goldman & Hewitt, 1976). High scorers on the math test choose science majors more often than do low scorers.

When school grades in different subjects are considered separately, the patterns of correlations indicate that somewhat different abilities influence different subjects (Thompson et al., 1978). For humanities and social sciences, verbal scores give much higher correlations with grades than do scores on other tests. For higher level mathematics (geometry, trigonometry, calculus), spatial tests, such as Spatial Reasoning on the *Differential Aptitude Test,* yield higher correlations with grades than do verbal tests (although the correlation of verbal tests with math achievement is still positive). Numerical tests yield high correlations with grades at all levels of math achievement, although at high levels the correlations are lowered because only the most numerically able students are still studying math at these levels. Grades in subjects such as physics, chemistry, and engineering yield higher correlations with mechanical aptitude tests than with verbal tests.

Success in various occupations is better predicted by some ability tests than by others (Ghiselli, 1966). Success in occupations involving direct verbal interactions with others, such as salesman, complaint clerk, receptionist, lawyer, and teacher, are more highly related to verbal tests than to tests of other abilities. Success in routine clerical jobs, such as secretary, typist, editor, and key punch operator, is best predicted by tests of speed and accuracy (Clerical Speed and Accuracy on the *Differential Aptitude Test*) while verbal scores also predict success in these jobs. Mechanical and spatial ability tests have the highest correlations with success involving servicing or repairing machinery, such as air conditioner repairman, plumber or carpenter.

Ability tests often correlate differently with learning a skill than with performing it after it is learned (Ghiselli, 1966). For example, spatial and mechanical abilities correlate well with training to be a fireman but not with proficiency on the job. Fleishman and Hempel (1955) have shown that throughout the acquisition of a skill the importance of various abilities changes. Initial steps in learning may be facilitated by quite different abilities than are required by skilled performance. For example, learning to play a first piano lesson depends greatly on finger dexterity and coordination while improvements at an advanced level depend more on sensitivity to small nuances and on artistic judgment (which is difficult to measure). The *Seashore Tests of Musical Ability,* for example, that measure very basic musical discriminations, predict early musical learning but not later skill.

Since the abilities involved at different stages of skill development are likely to vary, practical tests are usually constructed to be as similar to the criterion they are to predict as possible. If the criterion is completing a training program, the test constructor may choose items that require the subject to learn a similar task or at least test knowledge or skills that are prerequisite to the tasks to be learned. If the criterion is performance of a developed skill, say office management, the test may sample the subject's ability to cope with typical tasks. A problem may be presented by memo in an "in-basket" and the subject's completed response in the "out-basket" is scored. Although tests used practically tend to work better when they are very similar to the criterion, they mix together a wide variety of abilities in the same test, just as a wide variety of abilities will come into play from time to time in any job. Applied tests used for selecting people into specific jobs are, then, usually not very revealing about the specific abilities necessary to perform the jobs.

An educational consequence of different abilities that has been widely investigated is differences in learning between verbal and visual learners using either verbal or visual instructional techniques (Paivio, 1971). Students whose verbal ability scores are higher than their visual ability scores should learn more easily when information is presented verbally. Students with higher visual scores should learn most easily when information is presented graphically or by demonstration in order to take advantage of their stronger visual skills. The results of studies in this area are somewhat mixed (DeBoth & Dominowski, 1978; Delaney, 1978; Jensen, 1971).

While some evidence shows that verbal students perform better with verbal instruction and visual students with visual, the full effect seems to be masked by several factors. First, visual and verbal skills are positively correlated so that good visual learners are usually also good verbal learners and vice-versa. The correlation makes it difficult to identify really ideal cases of visual and verbal learners for comparison. Second, most subjects have been taught primarily verbally in the past. Teachers are well practiced in verbal presentation of their subjects, and students have more practice with verbal reception. Attempts to teach these subjects visually usually seem unnatural and awkward to teachers and students, making comparison difficult. Of course, the opposite applies to subjects such as geometry that require visual presentation. Third, even in experimental groups where the verbal or visual mode is emphasized, some of each almost certainly occurs in all groups. This makes comparisons between verbal teaching (with some visual) and visual teaching (with some verbal) less clear than we would like. Fourth, at the higher levels, students have mostly selected themselves into relatively verbal or visual subject areas, so that an attempt to teach, say, literature visually will find few visual learners enrolled to take advantage of the presentation. At present, we must conclude that if verbal and visual learners exist and do learn differently under different instructional conditions, the effect can be obscure without carefully controlled observation. Nevertheless, for unusual students with large discrepancies between verbal and visual abilities, assignment to the appropriate mode of instruction is likely to have positive effects.

USES OF COGNITIVE ABILITY

Ability tests have been widely used in a variety of settings, including clinical, educational, industrial, military, and counseling. They are used for diagnosis, selection, and assignment purposes in these settings, but the importance of the three purposes varies among the settings. Diagnosis is predominant in clincial settings and important in educational settings. Selection is the primary function of tests in industrial settings, as well as being important in military and educational settings. Assignment is the primary use of ability tests in educational and military settings while also being important in all the other settings. Ability tests used in counseling provide information that can allow clients to assign themselves to one of the available options (Schuerger & Watterson, 1977).

Diagnosis involves identifying a specific problem from test and other information available. In clincial settings, the diagnoses most clearly related to ability tests are neurological damage, dysfunction, or deterioration. To make judgments in this area, the clinician must compare the performances of the subject on several tests and look for patterns of scores associated with particular locations of brain functions. Information about the subject's background and sensory abilities must be considered since some test profiles associated with brain damage may also be associated with ethnic background. For example, higher scores on non-verbal tests and lower scores on verbal tests may indicate left-hemisphere damage, probable success in engineering, low socioeconomic status, or a sociopathic personality depending on information from sources other than specific ability tests. This pattern of scores could never mean all of these for the same person, although a clinician is likely to see all such cases from time to time. Motivation to take the tests must also be considered. Malingering can result from trying to avoid unpleasant tasks or trying to collect disability payments. It is possible to fake low scores on ability tests (although impossible to fake high scores).

Diagnosis in educational settings is largely associated with learning disabled children (Kirk & Kirk, 1971). These children have specific deficits that interfere with their school learning. By definition, they are normal in overall intelligence, so specific batteries of tests are used to try to distinguish their strong and weak abilities (cf. Friedman et al., 1977). After specific strengths and weaknesses are diagnosed, treatment programs are designed to exploit the strengths and improve the weaknesses.

Selection involves using tests and other information to identify persons who are highly likely to be successful at some particular activity. A great deal of research has been done concerning selection in industrial and military organizations. For positions with a large number of applicants and a relatively small number of openings, selection can result in overwhelming improvements in personnel decisions even with tests of only moderate validity. Success in most jobs can be predicted at least moderately well by some combination of ability, personality and interest tests (Ghiselli, 1966). Ability tests allow organizations to select the most productive people and avoid spending time and money training those who will probably not make a substantial contribution to the organization. This practice is quite profitable for the organization. It is also profitable for the people who are selected since they will not be refused an opportunity because the limited openings are filled with less competent people. Similarly, those who are not selected are not subject to periods of relatively unprofitable apprenticeship to occupations they will probably not attain and can spend this time doing something more promising for themselves. However, mistakes do occur, and selection must have negative effects on those who are mistakenly rejected.

Selection works in a similar manner for higher level educational institutions and for selective private schools at all levels. Using ability tests as well as other information, these schools choose only those who are most likely to succeed, and their graduates are in turn generally successful. For most of these schools, either verbal ability or general intelligence could be used for selection with approximately the same results. For technical, scientific, or engineering schools, tests of spatial, mechanical and numerical abilities are more appropriate.

Assignment involves placing a person in a setting where performance is likely to be better than it would be in other settings. Educational assessment using ability tests is primarily involved with answering the question, where or how will the child learn best? The distinction between visual and verbal learners, discussed previously, is a good example of using ability tests for assignment. The visual learner is assigned to a predominantly visual mode of teaching in which this stronger ability can be used to learn and not be hampered by the weaker ability. The opposite assignment is made for the verbal learner. Remedial work in the weaker ability may also be assigned.

Assignment using ability tests is used widely in industrial and even more widely in military settings. Where there are large numbers of persons who must be employed in some capacity, ability tests (along with other kinds of tests and information) are used to sort people into the specific activities where they are most likely to contribute to the organization's goals. A similar use is made of ability tests by vocational counselors, except that the goals of the client, rather than those of any organization are given priority. It must be noted that any given set of scores or ability tests can lead to very different decisions depending on whether the person's or the organization's goals have priority. For example, a person with very high verbal scores and only average mechanical scores would probably choose a verbal job of some sort. However, the personnel officer of a company (or other organization) with many mechanical and few verbal openings may assign this person to a mechanical job because of the probability that the person will do that job adequately and the company has less need for verbal skills. Goals, as well as abilities, dictate assignment and should be clearly stated to avoid confusion.

SUMMARY

Research and application of cognitive abilities have been reviewed. Different views of the structure of abilities have been discussed. Binet's view included only one factor of intelligence. Spearman called this factor "g" and measured other specific "s" factors along with it. Thomson viewed intelligence as composed of many small experiences in his sampling theory. Thurstone developed seven correlated primary mental abilities. Guilford elaborated a complex structure of intellect model based on contents, operations and products. Current research is converging on a view of mental abilities as a hierarchy with intelligence at the top. Intelligence includes verbal and spatial factors which in turn include additional subfactors. Physiological functions are the most likely causes of separate ability factors, and these ability factors contribute to a limited extent to educational and vocational choice and success. Ability tests are widely used in educational, clinical, military, industrial and counseling settings for diagnosis, selection and assignment.

CHAPTER 5

PERSONALITY

Personality refers to relatively stable, non-cognitive, differences in behavior. Unlike intelligence or cognitive abilities, personality is concerned with how people generally behave and not how well they are able to behave. Examples of personality characteristics are extraversion, anxiety, and impulsivity, to mention only a few.

Most early interest in personality was in psychiatric settings. Kretschmer (Eysenck & Eysenck, 1976) distinguished among psychotic patients along a dimension that closely resembles modern personality dimensions. Freud developed a complex personality theory involving dynamic interactions among the id, a primitive driving force, an ego, an egocentric entity, and a superego, roughly conscience. His theory was devised to explain the behavior of his mostly neurotic patients. Freud's writings have been extremely influential in psychology, particularly with regard to his notion that behavior need not be consciously motivated. Unfortunately, Freud stated his theory in a highly complex form without adequate measurement devices or specific observational criteria, thus leaving his theory difficult to test empirically. Those aspects of his theory that have been tested have generally not proved to be correct (Eysenck & Wilson, 1973). Nevertheless, the theory is widely applied in approximately its original form.

Scientific work in personality began when the measurement technology being developed for ability tests was applied to personality characteristics. Many of the primary researchers in personality such as Guilford, Cattell, and Eysenck are also important for their work with intelligence and abilities. It was clear that objective measures of clinically important characteristics other than abilities were needed. In the early part of this century personality assessment was highly subjective, depending on interviews and the patients' reactions to inkblots (the Rorschach test). Neither of these techniques produced results that were stable; in fact, neither produced results on which two clinicians could consistently agree. Just as with Freudian theory, these techniques are still widely applied.

These measurements yielded two very different kinds of results. One result was an explanation of the behavior of the patient in terms of the dynamism of the id, ego, superego, and perceived reality for the patient. None of these entities could be directly observed by clinicians, leaving open the possibility, indeed the likelihood, that two clinicians could construct two very different stories about the patient that were both highly convincing, at least within the context of the theory. While the first kind of assessment result was too complex to describe actual behavior, the second was too crude. This result involved assigning the patient to a category, such as schizophrenia or one of its subtypes or neurosis or one of its subtypes. These categories were (and still are) diagnosed as if they were diseases with single causes such as malaria. This style of diagnosis, called the medical model, produces results with low reliability because most cases are borderline in some sense—a little like this and a little like that (Lang, 1978).

Objectively measured personality characteristics are superior to both types of results. They are directly tied to objective measurement devices, thus avoiding the disagreements arising from Freudian statements. They do, however, often produce fairly complex results when the interrelations of various characteristics are considered. Also, measured personality characteristics are by their nature non-categorical. A person can score moderately high on two scales measuring very different characteristics and accurately be said to be a little like the first characteristic and a little like the second characteristic. Of course, cutoffs can be defined for the purpose of putting people into categories (and often are), thus recreating the problems of categorical diagnosis from non-categorical behavioral differences.

Quantitatively measured personality characteristics always show gradual differences from person to person in a population. If diagnostic categories were real (or accurately represented reality), we would expect to see, for instance on a schizophrenic scale, a large number of very low scores (not schizophrenics), a gap in the scores, and a smaller number of high scores (schizophrenics). In fact, what is found is a smooth distribution of scores from low, through middle (somewhat schizophrenic?), to high with most people falling in the middle or somewhat below. Using these scores it is easy to state the degree of this characteristic (schizophrenic responses) that a person shows. However, making a "yes" or "no" decision about whether a person belongs in the schizophrenic category is harder because the category itself is artificial.

An analogy can be drawn between personality assessment and intellectual assessment. Before intelligence tests were first used, the assessment of ability was categorical. There were mental defectives (including idiots, imbeciles, and morons), normals, and (following Galton) geniuses. After intelligence tests became widely used, the categorical system was mostly replaced by the continuous IQ score. Now the more quantitative terms, mental deficiency or (degree of) retardation, are preferred over the categorical term mental defective. The categorical sounding names that are still used in this area are simply rough verbal equivalents of the continuous scores. Of course, even with mental abilities, cutoffs may be defined as guides to treatment decisions, and we must continuously remind ourselves that the educable mentally retarded (EMRs) and the trainable mentally retarded (TMRs), for example, are only convenient classifications for treatment and communication purposes and are not discreet disease categories.

Several factors have made the acceptance of quantitative differences, rather than qualitative categorical distinctions, easier in the area of mental abilities than in personality. First, intelligence tests were constructed and used earlier than were personality tests. Also, intelligence tests measured people along a continuum that made important distinctions throughout its entire range—from profoundly retarded, through mildly retarded, through increasing levels of competence, to extremely gifted—while personality tests often are concerned with only one extreme tendency. For instance, a depression scale is usually used to distinguish severely depressed people from others, but almost never to identify the extremely underdepressed. Another historical factor is that personality theorists constructed highly elaborate verbal theories with categorical distinctions and hypothetical entities prior to objective personality measurement. Ability theorists, on the other hand, constructed their theories in conjunction with specific measurement devices.

The different structures of abilities and personality contribute to more quantitative thinking about abilities and more qualitative thinking about personality. The structure of, or interrelationships among, ability measures is relatively simple. All the tests correlate positively with each other making a one-dimensional framework from high IQ to low IQ the central factor. Human differences along this dimension are apparent to any observer even without a test, and the early diagnostic categories of abilities crudely reflected this quantitative dimension—idiot was lower than imbecile, which was lower than moron. Distinctions among subfactors of intelligence, such as verbal and spatial, are more recent and generally recognized to be subordinate to the central "g" factor.

Personality measures are not all positively correlated in the relatively simple manner that ability tests are. In fact, personality measures have several (about three) relatively independent factors (Eysenck & Eysenck, 1976) each of which has correlated subfactors analogous to the ability factors in intelligence. Without the aid of tests, observers of personality notice the qualitative differences among the various factors—say an anxious person versus a paranoid person—more than the quantitative differences along one factor—say a very anxious person and a moderately anxious one. These qualitative distinctions are correspondingly prevalent in personality theories. The more quantitative distinctions, such as schizoid (a little) versus schizophrenic (a lot), are more recent and still tend to be discussed in part as qualitative rather than completely quantitative differences.

During the last few decades, several groups of researchers have independently constructed personality questionnaires starting with different points of view and have come to a surprising degree of empirical (if not, theoretical) agreement. Two researchers, Eysenck and Cattell, started with diametrically opposed views and opposite approaches to factor analysis. Both constructed their questionnaires with Freud very much in mind. Cattell attempted to quantify Freudian theory and give it scientific respectability, while Eysenck opposed Freudian theory and has repeatedly provided evidence of the ineffectiveness of Freudian psychotherapy (Eysenck, 1952; Eysenck & Wilson, 1973). Their differences in factor analytic technique are too technical to be discussed here (see Eysenck & Eysenck, 1969) but can be briefly summarized by saying that Cattell identified a large number of correlated specific factors first and factored them to produce a smaller number of relatively independent general factors, while Eysenck initially measured the general independent factors. Despite their differences in orientation and technique, the general personality dimensions identified by Eysenck and Cattell are very similar (Eysenck & Eysenck, 1969). Eysenck and Cattell both identified Extraversion as a general dimension. Cattell's Anxiety and Eysenck's Neuroticism are approximately the same, and a refinement suggested by Gray (1973) may resolve what differences there are between them. Eysenck and Eysenck (1976) suggest a third dimension, Psychoticism, which is relatively independent of the first two. While clearly a concern in Cattell's work, Psychoticism is represented by several different factors.

A third group of researchers has constructed the *Minnesota Multiphasic Personality Inventory* (MMPI) (Marks, Seeman & Haller, 1974). The MMPI is by far the most widely used objective measure of personality. In fact, it is so extensively used that personality research and MMPI research are very close to synonymous. The construction of the MMPI differs drastically from that of Eysenck's or Cattell's measures. The MMPI was designed to be atheoretical, although its scales were named for clinical categories which derived from personality theory. Each scale on the MMPI is composed of items that discriminate between normals and patients in a particular abnormal category (e.g., hysterics). Each scale, however, produces a smooth distribution of scores rather than a cluster of normal scores separated from a cluster of abnormal scores. Although the MMPI was constructed without regard to theory using only the responses of normal and abnormal groups to select items, its results are very similar to those expected from Eysenck's theory (Wakefield, et al., 1974) as well as Cattell's (Cattell & Scheier, 1961).

Personality can be considered in the same hierarchical fashion that cognitive abilities have been (Eysenck & Eysenck, 1969). The important difference between abilities and personality is that three separate hierarchies are necessary for personality while only one is necessary for intelligence. Spatial and verbal abilities are substantially correlated components of intelligence, while the major personality dimensions are essentially uncorrelated. The three major personality dimensions are Extraversion, Neuroticism (also called emotionality or anxiety), and Psychoticism (also called toughmindedness) (Eysenck & Eysenck, 1976). Each of these is composed of correlated subfactors such as sociability and impulsivity.

Figure 5.1
Conceptual Placement of MMPI Scales in Eysenck's Personality Dimensions
(from Wakefield, et al, 1974)

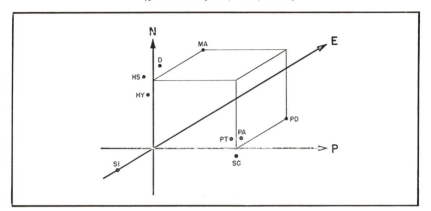

The first personality dimension, Extraversion, describes individual differences running from indifference toward other people (introverted behavior) through moderately sociable behavior which is characteristic of most people (ambiverted behavior), to highly sociable behavior (extraverted). This personality characteristic is considered normal throughout its range, although people at some points along the dimension may be better adapted in some settings than others. For example, an extraverted person would probably be happier and more successful as a salesman than would an introverted person of equal abilities. On the other hand, an introverted person would probably be better adapted to isolated work than would an extraverted person of equal abilities. Extraversion has been extensively researched (Wilson, 1978).

The second dimension, Neuroticism, can be thought of as nervousness or unhappiness. At one extreme of the dimension are people who are very unhappy or nervous for whom the term neurotic is an accurate description. At the other end are very calm, assured people for whom the term "stable" is used. Most people are somewhat in the middle of this range with moderate levels of nervousness, unhappiness, and self-doubt. High levels of neuroticism are the most frequent targets of treatment by most psychotherapists and behavior therapists.

The third dimension, Psychoticism, runs from warm, gentle, tender-minded behavior at one end to cold, aggressive, tough-minded behavior at the other. This dimension is called Psychoticism because people at the tough-minded end of the dimension have a higher frequency of psychotic breaks than those at the other end (Eysenck & Eysenck, 1976). The tough-minded end of this dimension has also been associated with creativity (Woody & Claridge, 1977) and may not be a negative or abnormal characteristic in all cases although disturbances associated with this dimension are often severe and resistant to treatment (Rahman & Eysenck, 1978).

Each of these dimensions is roughly independent of the others. This means that a person can have any level of the three characteristics in any combination (Wakefield, 1979). For example, an introvert can be either high or low on Neuroticism and high or low on Psychoticism. Introverts with different levels of Neuroticism and Psychoticism would behave very differently. Likewise, an extravert can be high or low on either of the other two dimensions. The number of possible combinations of the three personality dimensions is 27 if each dimension is divided into high, middle, and low scores (3 x 3 x 3), and many more when smaller differences are considered. This large number of combinations of levels of three dimensions accounts for a large amount of qualitative variation in personality from three quantitative dimensions.

Also, the three dimensions are essentially independent of intelligence, although small correlations may occur in some samples (particularly, negative correlations with Psychoticism). Each of the possible combinations of personality scores may be associated with any level of intelligence, thus making the qualitative variations in behavior even richer. There is, however, some evidence that cognitive abilities are somewhat related to the Extraversion dimension with extraverts tending to be higher on verbal ability and introverts higher on spatial (Riding & Dyer, 1980).

OBJECTIVE MEASUREMENT OF PERSONALITY

Three objective personality inventories will be discussed, although hundreds of questionnaires are currently available. The *Minnesota Multiphasic Personality Inventory* (MMPI) is considered because it is by far the most widely used objective personality measure. The *Eysenck Personality Questionnaire* (EPQ) is considered because it is the most direct measure of the three general personality dimensions. Cattell's *Sixteen Personality Factors Questionnaire* (16PF) is considered because it adds more specific details to the general factors.

The MMPI (Marks, Seeman, & Haller, 1974) was constructed during the 1940s to distinguish between various categories of psychiatric patients and normals. It has four "validity" scales to identify not answering items, lying, faking bad, and faking good along with 10 "clinical" scales which distinguish patients from normals, except for the *Mf* scale that distinguishes males from females and the SI scale that distinguishes (normal) introverts from other normals. The clinical scales are named after the groups of patients they identify. The scales are Hypochondriasis (Hs), Depression (D), Hysteria (Hy), Psychopathic Deviate (Pd), Masculinity-Femininity (Mf), Paranoia (Pa), Psychasthenia (Pt), Schizophrenia (Sc), Mania (Ma), and Social Introversion (SI). The interrelationships among the scales have been shown to conform with Eysenck's three-dimensional structure of personality (Wakefield, et a., 1974). While the MMPI is widely used in clinical settings, the abnormal item content and names of its scales make its use with normal groups questionable.

Also, the practice of scoring many of the items for more than one scale makes its use as a research instrument cumbersome (Wakefield, et al., 1975).

The EPQ (Eysenck & Eysenck, 1975) is the best choice for a research measure of personality. It has three scales called P, E, and N corresponding to the three dimensions and a lie scale. It has reliabilities in the .70s and .80s over short periods and reliabilities of about .70 over a 10 year period (Eysenck, personal communication, 1980) which is surprisingly high. The validity of this questionnaire has been established by its use (or the use of similar sets of items) in a wide variety of research (Eysenck, 1976). The Junior EPQ is a downward extension for children that is beginning to show its practical usefulness (Wakefield, 1979; McCord & Wakefield, 1981).

The 16PF and its various downward extensions for children (Cattell, Eber & Tatsuoka, 1970) provide scales that are in broad agreement with those on the EPQ as well as 16 more specific factors. Groups of these 16 factors are positively intercorrelated, thus producing the general personality factors. The construct validity of the scales of this questionnaire has been demonstrated by decades of research by Cattell and his colleagues. The 16PF is widely used with normal persons in counseling and vocational guidance settings (Schuerger & Watterson, 1977).

In addition to these objective measures of personality, it must be noted that there is a wide variety of non-objective sources of personality information that are frequently (if questionably) used in practical settings. Projective devices, such as the Rorschach, unstandardized behavioral observations (often in conjunction with an intelligence test or an interview), or simply "clincial intuition" are often cited as sources of personality information although the accuracy of this information has not been empirically established. When these sources of information are used (as they undoubtedly will continue to be) they should at least be confirmed by an established objective questionnaire.

CAUSES OF INDIVIDUAL DIFFERENCES IN PERSONALJTY

The debate over the causes of personality differences has involved fewer participants than has the debate over the causes of intellectual differences. Also, the personality debate has been conducted in professional journals rather than in newspapers and magazines. The debate over the causes of personality is broadly similar to the debate over the causes of intelligence. One group of researchers insists that environmental differences produce observed differences in behavior (e.g., Mischel, 1968). Another group of researchers has presented heritability analyses indicating substantial genetic-contributions to personality (e.g., Eysenck & Eysenck, 1976).

Personality is a structurally more complex area than is intelligence, and it is possible that on different dimensions of personality the genetic and environmental contributions are different. While intelligence and abilities are fairly tightly organized around one large factor, personality consists of three (and possibly more) independent dimensions. If intelligence is found to be predominently genetically caused, it is difficult to imagine that one of its components, say spatial ability, could be predominently environmental. Within the realm of personality, it would be possible to find that one dimension was predominently genetically caused and another mostly environmentally caused. Unfortunately, the debate is not conducted at this level, so that most writing has dealt with whether personality as a whole is genetically or environmentally caused.

What evidence is there that personality dimensions might be hereditary? First, several heritability analyses have been performed using the questionnaire results of persons with known percentages of shared genes—identical and fraternal twins, mostly (Gottesman, 1963; Eaves, 1973; Loehlin & Nichols, 1976). The data are not as extensive as they are for intelligence, but overall, it appears that almost half the variance of all personality dimensions is accounted for by heredity. This, of course, is a general statement. Gottesman (1963) found different heritabilities for the MMPI scales with higher heritabilities for social introversion and some psychotic scales, while Eysenck & Eysenck (1976) argue that, when corrected for unreliability, the heritability of psychoticism may be as high as 81 percent.

This argument is particularly important when we compare the heritabilities of personality dimensions with those of intelligence. It would be easy to conclude that intelligence, with typical heritabilities of .60 or over, is more genetically determined than personality, with typical heritabilities of just under .50. However, intelligence tests are much more reliable (high .90s) than are personality questionnaires (.70s and .80s, typically), and thus contain less measurement error. In heritability analyses, error is usually included with environmental effects. This artifactually lowers the heritability figures of personality questionnaires more than those of intelligence tests. Nevertheless, several psychologists (Vernon, 1953; Willerman, 1979) who have concluded that intelligence is largely hereditary have expressed doubts about the hereditary nature of personality.

Additional support for genetic contributions to personality has come from attempts to link personality dimensions to physiological structures. Eysenck (1967) linked extraversion to cortical arousal involving the reticular activating system in the brain stem and presented a substantial amount of experimental work supportive of this theory (Eysenck, 1976). Eysenck linked neuroticism to emotional arousability through the limbic system. Considering these two personality dimensions in relation to the stop-start or fight-flight mechanism, Gray (1973) hypothesized that extraversion should be related to responses to signals of praise or punishment. As Gray predicted, extraverted school children learn better under praising conditions and introverted school children under punishing conditions (McCord & Wakefield, 1981). This pattern of response has also been demonstrated with adult college students in India (Gupta & Nagpal, 1978).

The consistency of personality measures is a large concern in considering their causes (Eysenck & Eysenck, 1980). If personality measures had little or no stability over time, it could mean that momentary environmental pressures caused people to behave in one way in one situation and another in another situation (Mischel, 1968). Actually, lack of stability could mean several other things, including complex personality-situation interactions, simple lack of adequacy of the measures, or the operation of free-will. If personality measures are reasonably stable, this could mean that genetic traits consistently affect personality or that stable environments produce stable personalities. From these possibilities, it is clear that simply establishing the stability or lack of stability of personality questionnaires will not resolve the heredity-environment debate for personality.

It is surprising that the consistency of personality questionnaires became an issue, because their reliabilities over short periods of time (one month is typical) have been generally known to be near the .70s for decades. Mischel (1968) made this an issue by quoting validities (correlations of personality scores with other behavior) of .30, squaring them to get about .10, and claiming this figure as an index of the consistency of personality (Eysenck & Eysenck, 1980). Analyses of the reliabilities of personality questionnaires continue to give figures near the .70s, and analyses comparing the effects of personality variables and environmental variables on other behaviors indicate about equal contributions from both along with substantial, but not clearly defined, interactions between them (Wiggins, 1973). Of course, these substantial reliabilities for personality variables are not any more compelling evidence of the genetic causation of personality than the even higher reliabilities of intelligence tests are for the genetic causation of intelligence.

What evidence is there that personality is environmentally caused? To answer this question, we must distinguish between two levels of observation—specific responses and general dimensions. At the level of specific responses, there is overwhelming evidence (a) that behavior such as barpressing by rats and staying in a chair by school children can be environmentally manipulated and (b) that maintaining behavioral changes for long periods of time requires careful planning and consistent effort (Tharp & Wetzel, 1969). If behavior at this level represents personality (which is questionable), carefully manipulated environmental arrangements can have short-term effects on personality. The effects of naturally occurring environmental arrangements or long-term environmental effects of any kind on personality are less well established.

At the level of general personality dimensions (which is the level of observation at which the term personality is usually discussed), the picture is different. Environmental (in the form of therapeutic) effects are generally small and difficult to distinguish from changes that are made without intervention (Eysenck, 1952). In fact, abnormal subjects who do show improvement during therapy or hospitalization often show the same pattern of personality scores before and after treatment (Marks, Seeman, & Haller, 1975). In fact, most psychologists attempting to change behavior are outspoken in their contempt for general personality dimensions. Recognizing their inability to change these dimensions, they insist on specific behaviors as the appropriate level of observation for behavior change. The few attempts at environmental change at a general level, such as with shyness, aggression, or assertiveness, are still largely programmatic and their effectiveness is yet to be demonstrated.

A third possibility, that personality variables and environmental variables interact to produce behavior seems to be a stronger possibility in the area of personality than it is in the area of intelligence. In personality, large numbers of interactions have been reported (e.g. Magnusson & Endler, 1977) and practical applications suggested (Wakefield, 1979). Generally these interactions account for more of the variance in behavior than either personality or environment considered alone (Wiggins, 1973). This contrasts sharply with intelligence data that indicate that intelligence (and abilities) alone substantially predict performance, environment alone allows less accurate predictions, but the interactions between the two are relatively few and small. Matching each person with his own optimal environment is more promising using personality questionnaires than it is with intelligence tests.

Of course, the interactional approach does not resolve the question about the causes of personality. Even with large amounts of present behavior accounted for by interactions, there is still variance that may be directly attributable to environment or heredity independently. Currently, it appears that the independent contributions of these are approximately equal.

CONSEQUENCES OF PERSONALITY DIFFERENCES

Since personality encompasses several independent dimensions of behaviors, the consequences of differences on these dimensions are widely varied. The direct prediction of external behavior that can be made from any one personality dimension outside carefully controlled laboratory situations tends to be fairly small with correlations of about .30 being typical. When measures of all three major dimensions are used together or when measures of several smaller components of these dimenions, such as those in the 16PF, are used, the multiple correlations between personality and behavioral criteria are somewhat larger (Cattell, Eber & Tatsuoka, 1970). Particularly when the interaction between personality variables and situations or treatment conditions are considered, the prediction is greatly improved (McCord & Wakefield, 1981).

The first major personality dimension is extraversion (Eysenck, 1967). Persons who score high on measures of this dimension, that is extraverts, are typically sociable and impulsive. They like to be around other people and tend to seek out opportunities that will allow them to work with people, socialize frequently, and participate in groups rather than work alone. The extravert's motivation to achieve specific occupational or educational goals is typically low, but with the proper social pressures and encouragement the typical extravert may be more successful in achieving difficult goals than are others. Extraverts tend to perform better under conditions that allow them to take the lead and discover relationships for themself rather than simply follow directions. They also respond to praise more effectively than to criticism (Gray, 1972; Wilson, 1978).

Introverts tend to behave oppositely. They do not seek out other people and prefer to work alone. They also show a greater preference for recreation that allows them to be alone. They are cautious and respond to signs of negative consequences more than to signs of positive consequences (Gray, 1972). They are generally highly socialized to conform to rules and have fewer behavior problems than extraverted people (assuming intelligence and other personality characteristics are equal). They are also more highly motivated to achieve educational and occupational goals and achieve these most effectively with minimal external pressure to do so. External pressure tends to make them too aroused or tense to perform well (Wilson, 1978).

Figure 5.2
Arithmetic Achievement of Introverts and Extravers for Relatively Praising and Punishing Teachers (1 = most praising, 5 = most punishing)
(from McCord & Wakefield, 1981)

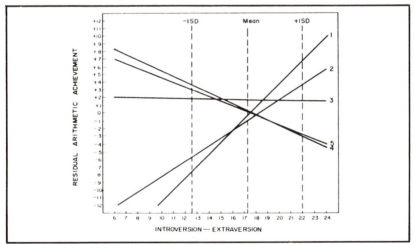

Of course, most people are somewhere between these two extremes. The term ambivert is often used for people with intermediate scores on extraversion-introversion measures. The behavior of these people is intermediate between the two extremes, although their behavior may be more like one or the other extreme depending on exactly where they fall on this dimension. Avoiding extremes, the behavior of ambiverts usually conforms more closely to the specific demands of the situation than that of extraverts or introverts.

The second dimension, neuroticism, is associated with unhappiness, nervousness, and psychological distress. People who have high scores on measures of this dimension are usually emotionally overreactive. They are often depressed or have a variety of bodily complaints. Under stress, they are likely to develop neurotic disorders, although in a non-stressful environment they may function adequately. These people are more likely to seek help from a psychologist, psychiatrist, or counselor than are other people. They may also seek help from physicians or clergymen if they are encouraged by others to view their distress as medical or religious in nature. This happens frequently since medical or religious problems are generally more acceptable than psychological problems. People who have lower scores on measures of neuroticism have much less psychological distress, are less likely to develop neurotic disorders, and are less emotionally reactive than those with higher scores (Eysenck, 1967).

Psychoticism, the third dimension, has been shown to be related to behavior problems, psychotic disorders, lack of warm feelings towards others, and arousal seeking (Eysenck & Eysenck, 1976; Friedman, et al., 1976). Persons with high scores on psychoticism or similar measures generally achieve less than others in school, have a higher incidence of behavior problems, and are more likely to have legal difficulties than are others. Although they are considered to be in need of therapy, they are not likely to seek it on their own and are often hostile toward therapy. In psychotherapy, they take longer and are less likely to achieve positive results than others, although certain drug treatments seem to be promising for these people (Rahman & Eysenck, 1978). On the other hand, people with high scores on psychoticism combined with high intellectual ability may be more creative than those with equal intellectual ability but lower scores on psychoticism (Woody & Claridge, 1977).

Personality variables give better predictions of behavior when they are used in combination with other information concerning the abilities of the person, his history, and his current situation (Wakefield, 1979). Since personality variables interact with each other and with environmental variables, statements of probable behavior from a single score on a personality questionnaire are much less accurate than those made from an intelligence score (although even these are best considered with other information). In combination, personality scores are much more useful, and several methods of combining personality scores for practical purposes are currently used.

The simplest way of combining personality scores is by cataloging all the possible combinations of scores. This may be further simplified by grouping scores together as high, middle, and low or just high and low depending on the variable and the purpose for which it is to be used. Wakefield (1979; McCord & Wakefield, 1981) has discussed scores from the *Eysenck Personality Questionnaire* in this manner. Separate statements of responses to various educational treatments have been made for each of 12 "combinations" of scores. The danger in this approach is that the combinations may be taken as diagnostic categories which they are not.

A similar approach to combining personality scores is interpreting profiles of scores rather than individual scores. This is the technique used with the *Minnesota Multiphasic Personality Inventory* (Marks, Seeman & Haller, 1974) which was originally constructed to identify abnormal clinical groups using one scale at a time. The scales are now usually referred to simply by a number (scale 4 rather than the Psychopathic Deviate scale) to encourage users to interpret profiles rather than individual scales. The results of this approach are similar to those of the combinations approach above. Profiles, like combinations, may inadvertently suggest diagnostic categories. The profiles or combinations are valuable when they are recognized as communication devices but detrimental when they are thought to be real categories. The categories are cruder and much less accurate than the continuous personality scores that are used to define them.

The most sophisticated way of combining personality information is with multiple regression. This technique combines the scores mathematically to predict a behavioral criterion without losing the continuous nature of the data. This is the approach used by Cattell (Cattell, Eber & Tatsuoka, 1970) with the 16PF. Equations are presented for predicting entry into and success in a large variety of occupations from the 16PF. Other equations predict behaviors such as marital stability using the personality scores of the husband and wife. While this approach is the most accurate, its acceptance is, for the moment, limited by the statistical skills of applied psychologists. A fairly complex formula must be used to predict each behavior of interest, and the accuracy of each formula, reflected by the multiple correlation, will be different. This approach requires more effort and skill than simply looking up a profile or combination to find the most likely consequences. Also, categories are simpler to present verbally in classroom settings than are regression formulas based on continuous scores.

Combining personality scores with a statistical technique similar to regression, Holder and Wankowski (1980) investigated the progress of more than 3000 university students in England through their undergraduate studies. Extraversion and neuroticism were related to entrance scores, the choice of subject studied, and success during the undergraduate years. Introverted students tended to study physical sciences, and extraverted students tended to study applied sciences (e.g., engineering). Students high on the neuroticism scale tended to study arts and social sciences. They interpreted these results as showing a theoretical bias for introverts, a practical bias for extraverts, and a "people-oriented" bias for high neuroticism scorers as well as for extraverts. Although there were some differences from subject to subject, the general trends in their results were that success was negatively related to neuroticism—that is high scorers failed more often than low scorers—and extraverted females and introverted males were more successful at their studies than were introverted females and extraverted males. However, since the extraversion variable was less strongly related to success for females than it was for males, introversion and low neuroticism generally were associated with success.

Similar results showing introverted males and extraverted females performing best in school is available for elementary school children (Naylor, 1972). This sex difference seems to occur throughout the school years. The overall relationship of extraversion and school performance, however, changes during the school years with extraverts having an advantage until about age 13 or 14 and introverts having an advantage thereafter. High neuroticism also appears to be more of a disadvantage earlier in school than it is later (Entwistle, 1972; 1979). A great deal of research into ways of dealing with neuroticism or anxiety is currently being done (Phillips, 1978).

As far as psychoticism and similar variables such as conduct disorders (c.f. Kohn, 1977) are concerned, high scores on these are consistently related to underachievement throughout the school years. These students achieve lower grades, drop out of school earlier, and require more discipline (usually with limited effectiveness) than their classmates with lower scores on psychoticism. Relatively punishing (or strict) teachers are more effective with these students (McCord & Wakefield, 1981), although actual physical punishment may lead to negative consequences for these students (Wakefield, 1979).

Vocational choice is also affected by personality just as is choice of subjects by university students (Ward, Cunningham, & Wakefield, 1976; Wakefield & Cunningham, 1975; Walsh, 1974). These relationships are consistent with Holland's (1973) theory of vocational choice based on the personality of the subject in relation to six types of occupations. Persons choosing Enterprising (sales mostly) jobs are assertive, conservative, and extraverted. Conventional (mostly clerical) jobs are chosen by relatively submissive, orderly people. Realistic (mechanical and outdoor) jobs go to those who are "thing-oriented" rather than "people-oriented." Investigative (scientific) jobs are filled mostly by introverted, perservering people. Artistic jobs are chosen by disorderly, creative, and aloof people. Finally, Social jobs are chosen by sensitive, emotional people. People tend to choose occupations at least partially by matching their personalities and needs with the requirements and qualifications they expect from various occupations. Those who make incorrect choices (based on their personalities) tend to be less satisfied with their jobs than are those who match their job better (Holland, 1973).

Besides educational and vocational consequences, personality variables have social consequences as well. There is a tendency for people to associate with others who are like themselves and even a slight tendency to marry others who are somewhat similar to themselves on some personality scales (Yom, et al., 1975). Afterwards, the stability and happiness of the marriage is related to the match between the personalities of the couple (Cattell, Eber & Tatsuoka, 1970; Eysenck & Wakefield, 1981). Personalities of parents (Bradley, et al., 1974) and of teachers (Wakefield, Cunningham & Edwards, 1975) influence their relationships with children and consequently have some influence on the children's behavior.

USES OF PERSONALITY VARIABLES

Personality variables are widely used in clincial, educational, vocational, and counseling settings. These variables have been used for diagnosis, selection, and assignment purposes, although diagnosis is their predominent use in clinical settings and assignment is predominent in the other settings. Personality questionnaires have often been used for selection purposes. However, it is difficult for people to accept being rejected on the basis of personality, since these questionnaires do not seem as clearly related to performance on a job or in school as do ability tests. In fact, their correlations with educational and vocational criteria are lower than those of ability tests. Consequently, personality questionnaires are used less frequently for selection than are ability tests.

Personality questionnaires are used most extensively in clinical settings. As we have seen, the MMPI was originally constructed to diagnose abnormal personality characteristics. Diagnosis (usually with the MMPI) is overwhelmingly the most frequent use of objectively measured personality characteristics in clinical settings. Distinguishing normals from psychotics and neurotics has been and continues to be a primary function of clinical psychologists and has clearly been a predominant force in shaping the study of human personality. In clinical practice, information other than objective questionnaires is also used to assess personality. Non-objective material such as interview data and responses to ambiguous stimuli (Rorschach cards) are widely used despite their low reliabilities and validities. Also, unstandardized and unvalidated objective data, such as observations of signs of personality during intelligence testing and observations of arbitrarily selected behavior, heavily influence personality assessment. In general, relationships between these observations and the subject's more important behavior in educational, vocational, and social settings have not been shown. These data should be used cautiously and only in conjunction with an objective, validated personality measure.

In vocational settings, it is often difficult to distinguish between personality measures and measures of vocational choice. Both types of questionnaires have been used for a long period and have produced generally similar information. The predominant theory guiding the work of most vocational counselors (Holland, 1973) holds that vocational choice is personality. Both types of questionnaires, along with ability tests, are used primarily for assignment, or more accurately, to assist a person to assign himself to an occupation.

In other counseling settings, personality is used in a similar manner to assist persons to make decisions (Schuerger & Watterson, 1977) or to put it another way to assist their self-assignment to various social situations. Marriage counselors may discuss similarities and dissimilarities in the personalities of their clients in order to allow them to anticipate problems and decide how to handle them. Clients in distressing situations (jobs, schools or relationships) may benefit by considering their personalities and needs in relation to the demands and gratifications of their current situation and of alternative situations.

Objective personality data have only recently come to be used in educational settings. The focus in education has been on intelligence and separate abilities. These tests have been widely and successfully used, overshadowing any concern with personality variables. Such attempts as have been made to use personality in the schools have usually depended on non-objective or unvalidated information and have been discouraging when compared to the results of ability testing. However, systematic use of personality questionnaires to individualize instruction is extremely promising (Wakefield, 1979). Assigning a student to optimal learning conditions based on known relationships between personality and performance can improve achievement substantially. Of course, intelligence, ability, and achievement tests are to be supplemented with, not replaced by, personality measures.

SUMMARY

Individual differences in personality have been reviewed. Personality refers to several, probably three, independent dimensions of behavioral differences, and their subfactors, that are relatively uncorrelated with intelligence. Currently, it appears that genetic and environment factors contribute about equally to individual differences in personality. Personality differences and situational variables contribute about equally to differences in a variety of behaviors but are both less important than the interactions between them. Personality differences influence a variety of important educational, vocational, and social behaviors, and personality questionnaires are widely used in most applied psychological settings.

CHAPTER 6

CREATIVITY

Identifying creative persons has been a concern of psychologists studying individual differences since Galton's work in the late 1800s. In fact, in the early work, the search for creativity was the central concern. When Galton studied "eminent" men and tried to measure "genius," he made no distinction between what we now call intelligence and what we now call creativity; "genius" or "eminence" included both. Creativity might simply have been conceived as very high levels of intelligence (to use the modern terms).

Galton (1874) did not need a distinction between creativity and intelligence since he was primarily concerned with people who had already made outstanding contributions to society. The men he considered in his *Hereditary Genius* (Galton, 1924) were those who had written, invented, discovered, or theorized in different areas. It would be safe to say that all these men, such as Galton's cousin Charles Darwin, the discoverer of evolution, were both highly intelligent and highly creative. People who were intelligent, but not creative, or creative, but not intelligent, were very unlikely to come to Galton's attention.

The first hint that there might be a distinction between the two concepts arose in Binet's work. Binet focused on the lower levels of intelligence while Galton focused on the higher levels. Also Galton's subjects were generally adults who had already achieved eminence, while Binet's subjects were children who had not yet had the opportunity to achieve. A person had to be both highly intelligent and highly creative to qualify for Galton's term eminent. Binet, on the other hand, simply wanted to distinguish those children who could not benefit from school from those who could. He tried several kinds of items on his test to see which would make this distinction, including some items that required original responses and others that required "correct" answers. The items requiring original responses failed to distinguish between the students who were rated successful by their teachers and those who were rated unsuccessful, and therefore were eliminated from the test. They did not work for the practical task of identifying students in need of special help. On the other hand, many of the items requiring established correct answers (which of course could not be original) did distinguish between the poor students and the adequate students and were retained on Binet's intelligence test. Similar items are included in current intelligence tests.

Intelligence tests constructed since Binet's time do not generally include items requiring originality or creativity. In fact, persons with a strong tendency to give unusual responses or to be too thoughtful when answering items on an intelligence test may find themselves at a disadvantage when compared to a person who quickly gives a widely accepted "correct" answer without a great deal of deliberation (Glasser & Zimmeman, 1967). Intelligence tests are widely criticized for failing to include creative items. Nevertheless, inclusion of these items, which are generally irrelevant to academic achievement, would reduce the effectiveness of intelligence tests for identifying students needing special help to succeed in school. Perhaps a more relevant criticism might be directed at academic achievement. Is it appropriate that academic achievement and creativity should be unrelated?

A study by Getzels and Jackson (1962) illustrates the differences between creative students and intelligent students. Using a variety of tests, these investigators divided a sample of gifted students into two groups: (a) high intelligence and low creativity and (b) low intelligence and high creativity. Although teachers may proclaim their interest in creativity in the abstract, their ratings of their students indicated that they did not like creative students in the flesh. These students disrupted their activities, and caused the teachers extra work, frustration, and often embarrassment. They very much preferred intelligent students to creative students. The intelligent students were compliant, quick to learn, and far more pleasant for the teachers. The ratings of other students showed a familiar irritation with creative students, although they did often find them entertaining.

Although this study has been criticized for artificially magnifying the distinction between creativity and intelligence, it does indicate that when these traits are carefully distinguished their effects on their owners' behavior and the reactions of others to these persons are quite different. In general it seems that high intelligence is valued by teachers, peers, and its possessor during its development as well as in maturity. High creativity, on the other hand, often leads to difficulties with authority and peers during its development and consequently is only valued after its possessor has produced something clearly creative in maturity.

WHAT IS CREATIVITY?

The difference between the positive value attributed to creative products—such as scientific discoveries, inventions, and works of art, as well as to creativity in the abstract—and the negative value attributed to the often troublesome behavior of creative persons during their development has led to different ways of conceptualizing creativity (c.f., Dellas & Gaier, 1970; Welsh,

1975). Three different approaches to creativity can be identified. The first approach reflecting the positive value views creativity as simply high intelligence. The second views creativity as a cognitive ability (or abilities) distinguishable from other abilities. The third approach influenced by the observations of the troublesome behavior of creative persons views creativity as the result of one or more personality variables combined with intelligence.

Creativity viewed as high intelligence was the first way it was discussed scientifically. In fact, Galton's work may be better considered as dealing with what we now call creativity than with what we now call intelligence. In the 1800s, scientific progress was widely evident. New discoveries and inventions occurred almost daily, and Galton was very concerned with identifying persons who would produce more discoveries. Since there were not as many highly technical occupations then as there are now, sheer ability to learn, retain, and use information in more or less standard ways was not as valuable as it is now. Learning ability (or intelligence) was then simply a prerequisite for creative production. Certainly some minimal level of intelligence was required to allow a person to learn enough information so it could be combined in unusual ways or used to find completely new information, but learning ability itself was not the central concern. Later, as more jobs required greater learning ability (but not necessarily creativity), intelligence became more important than creativity for an overwhelming majority of people. For most people, there is little point in predicting whether they will produce a highly creative product since very few people do, but predicting whether they can learn fast enough and well enough to perform a technical or professional job has become increasingly important during this century. Consequently, a great deal of effort has been made to measure intelligence (without considering creativity) and much less effort has been given to measuring creativity (with or without considering intelligence).

The idea that high creativity and high intelligence are either the same or similar has influenced the research on both topics as well as the practical use of the concepts. Several tests of creativity can be described as simply very hard intelligence tests requiring the person taking the test to produce one correct answer in response to some information. The *Remote Associates Test* (Mednick & Mednick, 1967) is the best example. It is not surprising that this test correlates highly with intelligence tests and particularly with their verbal parts. McNemar (1964) suggested a slight modification of the idea that intelligence and creativity are the same. He suggested that they are the same (or at least highly correlated) up to a certain level, perhaps IQ 120, and beyond that point are distinct (or have a lower correlation). This "fan-shaped" hypothesis clearly considers intelligence as a prerequisite for creativity. Low levels of intelligence limit persons to low levels of creativity. Moderate levels of intelligence allow moderate creativity. High levels of intelligence allow high levels of creativity but do not guarantee high levels of creativity. In other words it is possible for a person with an IQ of 140 to be either highly creative or not, but a person with an IQ of 80 will definitely not be creative. Studies evaluating this hypothesis have, however, generally shown that IQ and creativity are similarly correlated (at a moderate level) throughout their ranges (Mednick & Andrews, 1967). These results indicate that a person's levels of intelligence and creativity are similar: that is, a person will tend to be either high on both or low on both.

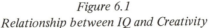

Figure 6.1
Relationship between IQ and Creativity

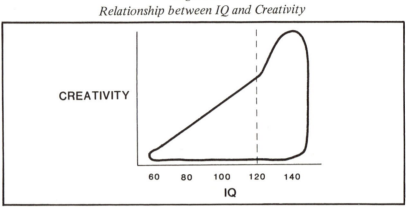

In practical efforts to identify gifted children, creativity is used as the justification but intelligence tests are the measures usually used for identification. Most laws mandating special services to nurture outstanding talent attempt to include talent in all artistic and intellectual areas. These laws are designed to identify creative students and to foster their creativity. However, a limit (commonly 2 percent of the population) is usually imposed for budgetary reasons requiring a standard competitive measure to determine which children qualify for the special services. Since it is impossible to compare, say, musical talent with scientific promise, an intelligence test is generally used as a common denominator. To the extent that intelligence and creativity are correlated, this would be an adequate practice. However, the correlation is not exceedingly high, with about .4 being typical.

Another possibility is that creativity is reflected in one or more cognitive abilities that can be distinguished from general intelligence but are correlated with general intelligence. Most work on creativity has followed this approach. Guilford (1979) has identified several divergent production abilities as indicative of creativity. Tests of these abilities require the subject to think of new possibilities or alternatives when presented with some information. These abilities are contrasted with convergent abilities which require one correct answer. Convergent abilities are emphasized in school work and intelligence tests designed to predict school work. Divergent abilities reflect creativity and are currently not encouraged (and are probably discouraged) in typical educational activities. Other workers have also concentrated on measuring creativity through unusual responses or fluency of responses (Torrance, 1962) as opposed to the correct responses typical of intelligence tests. These tests are only moderately related to intelligence as we would expect of tests of separate abilities. Unfortunately, they are not highly correlated among themselves suggesting that they do not all measure the same "creativity."

The possible existence of separate creative abilities has led to suggestions (Wallas, 1926; Osborn, 1953) that these abilities should be used in a certain order to maximize creativity. The first step toward a creative product is immersing oneself in information available in an area. This requires a reasonable level of learning ability and is consistent with treating intelligence as a prerequisite to creativity. The second step is called incubation. During this time, the creative person does not attend to the problem. The information learned is allowed to recombine in ways that it might not if an answer to the problem were forced. In order to produce unusual solutions, the person must try not to solve the problem too quickly. Forced solutions are likely to be reasonable and even correct, but not creative. Next, the creative person produces a large number of possible solutions without prejudging the solutions. There must be a willingness to entertain absurd possibilities. A creative solution may initially appear absurd because it is not the usual, correct sort of solution to the problem. Prematurely judging solutions will result in virtually all creative solutions being quickly discarded. Finally, the solutions produced must be evaluated. The valuable creative solutions must be selected from the rest, but only after the production of many possibilities.

The third approach to creativity takes as its starting point the apparently maladjusted behavior of many creative persons. Particularly among artists, bizarre behavior has become an entrenched part of the stereotype—crazy artists are expected; happy, well-adjusted artists are surprising. Also, creative scientific workers often seem maladjusted (e.g. Newton), unmotivated (e.g. Darwin), or academically deficient (e.g. Einstein). A large number of studies have compared creative persons with others (Barron, 1969). In general, creative persons are more introverted than other people and higher on virtually all measures of psychopathology. They also are higher on several positive traits such as flexibility, self-acceptance, and dominance. Barron (1963) has concluded that creative persons are ". . . more troubled psychologically, but they also have far greater resources with which to deal with their troubles."

In terms of the three-dimensional view of personality presented earlier, the highly creative person is usually introverted, high on neuroticism (but not necessarily a neurotic), and high on psychoticism (but probably not a psychotic) (Wakefield & Goad, 1981). Of the three traits, the one that has received the most attention in creativity research has been psychoticism, as well as related measures such as the schizophrenia scale of the MMPI. It seems strange that creative persons score high on the schizophrenia scale since clinical schizophrenics are far from creative (unless one adopts a perverse definition of creativity). What creatives and psychotics have in common is flexibility, impulsivity, and a resistance to easy acceptance of socially approved "correct" behaviors and modes of thought. Creative persons are able to make use of these characteristics, although they occasionally cause trouble for themselves, while psychotics are unable to control these characteristics and may find themselves institutionalized (Woody & Claridge, 1977).

The difference between creatives and psychotics is at least as important as their similarities. The difference between them is primarily intelligence. The "greater resources" that creatives have to deal with their "troubles" (in Barron's terms) are shown on an intelligence test. Clinical psychotics are usually subnormal on intelligence (although some have a history of higher performance). Their flexibility of thinking combined with limited intellectual ability sounds abnormal and severely limits their prospects for even minimal adjustment to society much less significant contributions to it. Persons recognized for their creativity are virtually always above average in intelligence, although their IQs in some cases are not extremely high. Flexible thinking combined with high intelligence allows these people to avoid being limited by social conventions but in productive rather than pathological ways. They are able to contribute to and change these conventions, while an intelligent person who is lower on psychoticism typically works within the conventions very efficiently but changes them very little.

All three views of creativity give a central role to intelligence in explaining creative behavior. In the first view, creativity without at least a moderately high level of intelligence does not seem to be possible; in other words, intelligence limits creativity because the two are essentially identical. In the second view, intelligence limits creativity in that creative abilities are components of general intelligence that must be used along with other abilities in order to allow creative behavior. In the third view, intelligence limits creativity because creative personality characteristics in the absence of high intelligence are pathological rather than creative.

MEASUREMENT OF CREATIVITY

Although there are three approaches to creativity, most tests of creativity have been constructed as tests of separate creative abilities, the second approach discussed above. This approach is more conducive to constructing tests called creativity tests than are the other two, in that this approach assumes that creative abilities exist in a distinct measurable form. The view of creativity as high intelligence does not encourage the construction of separate creativity tests; intelligence tests themselves are used for assessing creativity. The view of creativity as a personality characteristic combined with high intelligence also does not encourage the construction of separate creativity tests; established personality questionnaires and intelligence are used instead.

The most widely discussed measures of creativity are Guilford's (1979) tests of divergent production. These tests are contrasted with tests of convergent production that require standard correct answers. Divergent production tests allow the subject to give numerous unusual answers that can all receive high scores although none is *the* correct answer. These tests have been constructed in the context of Guilford's Structure of Intellect (SOI) model that has been discussed previously. Divergent production is one of the operations in this model that must be considered along with the various contents and products included in the model. When all the contents and products on which the divergent production operation can be performed are considered, several tests are possible and have actually been constructed. These tests of creativity are all correlated with each other and correlated at lower levels with other tests in the SOI model.

Another test of creativity is the *Remote Associates Test* (RAT) (Mednick & Mednick, 1967). In this test, the subject is asked to form associative elements into new combinations. The elements are three words that are apparently unrelated but are all associated with one other word. This common associated word is the correct answer. This test appears to be a difficult test of verbal skills and in fact correlates in the .40s with other tests of verbal abilities and intelligence.

The *Minnesota Tests of Creative Thinking* (MTCT) (Torrance, 1962) provide separate measures of verbal and non-verbal (visual) creativity. These two measures are largely uncorrelated with each other, but they are highly correlated with intelligence tests (Welsh, 1975). In fact, one investigator (Yamamoto, 1965) showed that the MTCT correlated .88 with the *Lorge-Thorndike Intelligence Test* after making statistical corrections for restriction of range in the sample. If this correlation is correct, intelligence as measured by the Lorge-Thorndike and creativity as measured by the MTCT are virtually identical.

All three of these creativity tests show the pattern of correlations that has come to be expected from tests of separate cognitive abilities. That is, they correlate positively with tests of other abilities and with general intelligence tests. Their correlations with each other, however, are generally too small to justify considering them all as measures of one creative ability. Particularly verbal tests of creativity and visual tests of creativity are unrelated. This suggests that a person may be verbally creative but visually uncreative, or vice-versa.

CAUSES OF CREATIVITY

While the heredity-environment question has emerged in the study of creativity (MacKinnon, 1962), the causes of creativity are, to a large extent, determined by our view of what creativity is. If we were to choose one of the three general approaches to creativity as the most likely to be correct, a separate discussion of the causes of creativity would be unnecessary. This is especially the case if the view of creativity as high intelligence is adopted. To the extent that this approach is true, the causes of creativity and intelligence are identical. In fact, the heritabilities of creativity test scores computed from data on monozygotic and dizygotic twins are approximately the same as the heritabilities of intelligence, ranging from about 55 percent inherited to about 78 percent inherited (Barron, 1969).

Of course, these heritabilities are not inconsistent with the other two approaches to creativity. If creativity is one or more separate cognitive abilities, we might also expect heritabilities in this range. Other separate abilities (e.g. spatial abilities) have high heritabilities, and it would not be inconsistent for separate creative abilities to show similarly high heritabilities.

Likewise, personality characteristics appear to be substantially inherited allowing the heritabilities reported to be considered reasonable within the view of creativity as a combination of personality and intelligence. It is even possible that if creative persons mate with each other the personality and intelligence characteristics of each, that in combination produce creativity, may lead to other possibilities in their offspring (Karlsson, 1978). Some may be highly intelligent but lacking the personality characteristics leading to creativity. These should, in general, lead relatively successful but unremarkable lives. Some may inherit the personality characteristics (i.e. the psychotic and schizophrenic tendencies) without the high intelligence. Of course, some may inherit both relevant characteristics and become creative. All of these possible offspring are good candidates for institutionalization—in professional schools, mental wards, and graduate schools, respectively.

The effect of environment on creativity has been widely discussed (Taylor & Barron, 1963) although efforts to increase creativity have not been as extensive as efforts to identify the creative. It is difficult to state how much effect environmental conditions have on creativity or how much they might have if the proper conditions were known. Whatever effect the environment has on creativity at the current time is probably a supressing effect (Barron, 1969). Unusual responses in school are usually considered silly or undisciplined rather than creative and tend to be punished. Correct responses are encouraged. This supression of creativity may account for the rarity of truly creative individuals.

Programs for nuturing creativity are widespread (Torrance, 1962; Rogers, 1959). They typically suggest that children be given greater freedom to explore and that the teacher accept unusual responses without corrections. There is no evidence that such programs actually have any effect on creativity. Attempts to positively reward unusual responses are usually limited to short-term experimental manipulations producing only small immediate effects without evidence of generalization. All such efforts at enhancing creativity are limited by the difficulty of defining exactly what creativity is and what the relative values of creativity and (correct) learning are. Since learning is at least as highly valued as creativity (and perhaps more so) and is easier to measure, learning is usually emphasized over creativity in educational programs.

CONSEQUENCES OF CREATIVITY

The immediate consequences of creativity for both children (Getzels & Jackson, 1962) and adults (Barron, 1969) are well documented. At both age levels, creative persons are judged to be more intelligent than average, although not necessarily more intelligent than comparison persons chosen for high intelligence but low creativity. Creative persons offer relatively large numbers of ideas of varying quality; they offer both good and bad ideas (as judged by others) frequently. In fact, their tendency to consider what are later seen to be bad ideas frequently is a source of irritation to others. Of course, they more frequently offer the rare good ideas as well.

These observations are consistent with the view that includes intelligence as a prerequisite of creativity. Moderately high intelligence is required for a person to produce creative ideas, but high intelligence does not seem to guarantee creativity. Other creative abilities are necessary in addition to high intelligence. The most obvious ability involved has been called divergent production or simply fluency. The ability to combine information in unusual ways is also required.

Creative persons appear to have certain personality characteristics more frequently than do other people. They are more anxious, more impulsive, more maladjusted, more introverted, and more dominant than others (Barron, 1969). No doubt some of these characteristics are consequences of creativity and others are causes or simply components of creativity. Which are causes and which are consequences is difficult to determine with the research that has been done. High anxiety could be either a driving force behind creativity consistent with its frequently mentioned motivational properties (e.g. Wakefield, 1979) or a result of critical reactions of others to the unusual ideas presented by the creative person. Similarly, the creative person's introversion could be a characteristic that allows the individual to avoid high exposure to "usual" ideas and thereby produce "unusual" ideas. On the other hand, introversion could be a consequence of the creative person's being rejected by others and thus rejecting others in return. Dominance (Barron, 1969) and impulsivity (Woody & Claridge, 1977) are likely to be either causes or components of creativity that allow the creative person to consider and present ideas without prematurely rejecting them. Either of these could be, to some extent, a consequence of creative persons' strong efforts to resist suppression of their ideas by others. These efforts might take the form of feelings of superiority (dominance) or attempts to present ideas quickly before competitive ideas appear (impulsivity).

The frequent maladjustment of creative persons is almost certainly a consequence of creativity. The creative person's refusal to accept conventional behaviors and solutions to problems may result in ostracism from many social activities. Creative persons tend to disregard rules and norms at school and later at work, preferring to try to do things their own way. These attempts are irritating to others when they fail and may be costly or disruptive.

When the attempts are successful, they may very well elicit jealousy from the creative person's peers. Of course, other characteristics (anxiety, impulsivity, introversion) that may have been evident in the creative person since early years may be increased by the maladjustment resulting from creative efforts. These characteristics may constitute parts of a positive feedback system with creativity; persons with higher anxiety, impulsivity, or introversion may attempt more creative behavior leading to more maladjustment and eventually higher levels of anxiety, impulsivity, or introversion.

Long term effects of creativity are not as well documented. Since truly creative achievements in art or science are relatively rare in the population, their accurate prediction by empirical methods is impossible (Wiggins, 1973). The construction of tests that would accurately predict which children will create new scientific theories or new works of art in maturity simply will not happen. However, combinations of personality, intelligence, and creative ability tests already in use can identify a relatively small proportion (say 10 percent) of children as those most likely to be creative. From this group, virtually all of the very rare creative events will arise, even though most of the group will not produce highly creative products (Taylor & Holland, 1964).

USES OF CREATIVITY

Creativity tests are used primarily in educational settings and in industrial settings for selecting among applicants for high level managerial positions. In both settings creativity tests serve only a screening function and are used along with other instruments to include creative talent in the selected group.

In educational settings, the concept of creativity (probably more than the tests for creativity) has emphasized that original responses are stifled in programs that focus on learning "correct" information. Disciplinary problems may result from the struggle between the child's creative attempts and the teacher's attempts to teach in an orderly fashion. Children with creative promise may be identified and their original responses encouraged and a certain amount of productive disorder allowed. Of course, creativity tests do not (and never will) accurately identify exactly which students will achieve high levels of (very rare) creative production. The best that can be hoped for is that a promising student will be identified as potentially creative and given encouragement rather than being considered disruptive and subjected to stricter controls.

In selecting for creative talent in industry (or in higher education), the appropriate goal is to include those with creative talent in the group selected rather than to assure that every person in the selected group is highly creative. A company with only creative managers would probably fall apart from massive lack of cooperation, while one with some creative managers among a large number of competent (but less creative) managers will have the right combination of new ideas and competent execution of ideas. A company with no creative managers is likely to stagnate. Similarly, universities must include creative talents in the groups being trained, but not every individual must be highly creative. Competent, careful work must occur side by side with revolutionary creative achievements.

Other settings in which routine (assembly line work) or discipline (the military) is essential are likely to find little use for creativity tests. They are not currently used in these settings.

SUMMARY

Three views of creativity have been presented: creativity as high levels of intelligence, creativity as separate cognitive abilities, and creativity as a combination of high intelligence and certain personality characteristics (particularly psychoticism). Specific measures of creativity have mostly come from the search for cognitive creative abilities. The causes of creativity are similar to the causes of the individual differences that are components of creativity. Some evidence of heritability of creativity is available, although the components of creativity may be separately inherited rather than inherited together. High levels of creativity result in a high frequency of both good and bad ideas (fluency) and unusual ideas that occasionally are judged creative. Maladjustment and associated personality characteristics may also be related to creative behavior.

CHAPTER 7
COGNITIVE STYLES

Research on cognitive styles began in the 1950s (Witkin, et al., 1954) as a result of observations of individual differences in responses to perceptual tasks in experimental settings. Some people were very accurate at these tasks and some were less accurate, and the differences were not strongly related to intelligence. Also, different subjects seemed to use different information to respond to the tasks. Some appeared to respond primarily on the basis of cues from the stimulus and others responded to other cues, particularly social cues and cues from the background. These observations led to the study of Field Independence versus Field Dependence which was the first cognitive style variable. Subjects who responded to stimulus cues primarily were said to be field independent. Those who were more influenced by background and social cues were said to be field dependent.

Field independent and field dependent persons are identified with several tasks. One is the Rod and Frame Task, that requires a subject to adjust a luminous rod to the vertical position while in a completely dark room. A luminous frame around the rod will have been previously adjusted by the experimenter to give misleading cues. A field independent person adjusts the rod accurately while a field dependent person is influenced by the frame and incorrectly adjusts the rod. A field independent person can also identify figures embedded in complex designs more accurately than can a field dependent person. While the measurement of this difference in style is limited to a few specific tasks, field independence-field dependence is related to a wide range of intellectual and educational differences, (Witkin, Moore, Goodenough & Cox, 1977) as well as with differences in interpersonal behavior (Witkin & Goodenough, 1977).

Although field independence is the oldest and most widely researched cognitive style, other cognitive style variables have been investigated. The next most widely researched variable is Reflection versus Impulsivity (Kagan & Kogan, 1970. This variable is concerned with how long a subject will delay a response in an uncertain situation while considering the possible responses.

Reflective subjects delay this response longer and usually make fewer errors than impulsive subjects. This variable also is related to a wide range of personality and educational characteristics (Messer, 1976).

Other cognitive style variables are broad versus narrow breadth of categorization (Pettigrew, 1958), styles of conceptualization (analytic, categorical, and relational) (Kagan, Moss & Sigel, 1963), complexity versus simplicity (Kelley, 1955), focusing versus scanning (Guilford, 1980), analytical versus global (Wachtel, 1968), and leveling versus sharpening (Gardiner, et al., 1959). All of these variables refer to characteristic ways people approach problems and take in information to solve the problems. As can be seen from their names, there is some similarity among the various cognitive style distinctions. For instance an analytical person tends to be more reflective and field independent, and a global person, more impulsive and field dependent. In fact, terms from one area of research are frequently used to describe distinctions in other areas (cf. Kagan, et al., 1964), and evidence is gradually accumulating (Banta, 1970; Massari, 1975), showing that some of the cognitive style variables are substantially correlated.

From the beginning of the study of cognitive styles, these variables have occupied a conceptual "half-way house" (Guilford, 1980) between personality variables and intelligence or ability variables. Some researchers have considered these variables as closely related to personality (Witkin, et al., 1954; Witkin & Goodenough, 1977; Vernon, 1973), and others (Broverman, 1960; Messick, 1976; Guilford, 1980) have treated them as intellectual variables. Kogan (1976) has systematically considered the conceptual relationships between abilities, personality, and cognitive styles. He divides cognitive styles into three types. Type I is closest to abilities in that these variables are measured with tests that have correct (or accurate) and incorrect (or inaccurate) responses. Field Independence is a Type I cognitive style. Type II cognitive styles are measured without considering the accuracy of the response, but the investigators place greater value on one style of performance than another. The analytic style, while not more "correct" than the thematic-relational style, is considered more advanced by its investigators (Kagan, Moss & Sigel, 1963). Type III cognitive styles are value-neutral differences and farthest from the ability domain. Broad categorizers and narrow categorizers function differently but neither seems to have an overall advantage over the other (Kogan, 1971). It is interesting that in Kogan's three types, the value attached to a cognitive style is exactly the same as its relation to abilities.

Some researchers have viewed cognitive styles as cognitive controls or intellectual executive functions (Guilford, 1980). This view suggests that cognitive styles are abilities that dictate which strategy a person will employ to solve a particular problem. Especially when distinctions such as verbal versus visual or divergent thinking versus convergent thinking are discussed as cognitive (or sometimes learning) styles, it seems quite reasonable that a person may consistently try to apply stronger abilities to any new problem that occurs resulting in a certain "style" of problem solution. Perhaps spatial abilities dictate whether a person will scan for information or focus on a likely detail, or perhaps memory limitations determine the degree of complexity in a person's information seeking.

Alternatively, personality differences may result in cognitive styles which in turn control the application of a person's abilities. Anxiety has been used frequently to explain differences in reflection-impulsivity (Kogan, 1976) although in somewhat different ways. The simplest explanation is that the reflective subject is high in anxiety over error, resulting in cautious responding, while the impulsive subject is low in anxiety and gives quick careless responses. This view is strikingly similar to Gray's (1970) theory that introverts, who share many characteristics with reflectives, learn better than extraverts, who are similar to impulsives, in situations involving punishment (i.e. responding incorrectly). Reflection-impulsivity and the personality variable introversion-extraversion are generally very similar (Guilford, 1980) as can be seen by comparing the introvert's thoughtful, reserved, serious behavior with the same behaviors of reflective subjects (Wakefield, 1979) and by considering the impulsive behavior of extraverts (Eysenck & Eysenck, 1977).

Wardell and Royce (1978) view styles as moderators that link cognitive and affective traits. In this view, styles are intermediate between abilities and personality (affective) traits. Cognitive styles have been influenced by both psychoanalytic ego psychology (under the term ego controls) and experimental cognitive psychology and should be expected to occupy a position influencing both affective and cognitive traits. In most cases, a person's abilities and personality should be consistent, and cognitive styles will reflect this. For example, a person with an extraverted, energetic personality might learn quickly and have fast reactions, but limited patience with prolonged tasks. Such a person would have an impulsive, global field-dependent cognitive style consistent with his or her personality and abilities. Of course, the possibility exists that an individual's personality and abilities will not be consistent, resulting in an unusual cognitive style balancing and moderating between the inconsistencies.

WHAT ARE COGNITIVE STYLES?

In most discussions, cognitive styles are treated as personality variables and ability variables simultaneously (Guilford, 1980). They have been viewed as ego controls or a result of anxiety, suggesting that they are personality variables. They are also viewed as controlling intellectual processes, which is the reason for the continuing interest in these variables. By virtue of controlling cognitive processes (and because they are often measured by tests with correct and incorrect responses), cognitive styles are often included in the ability domain.

Especially with the two most widely researched styles—field independence-dependence and reflection-impulsivity—there is research indicating correlations with both personality and ability variables. Impulsivity (Messer, 1976) is related to several clinical disorders associated with lower intellectual performance, including hyperactivity, brain damage, epilepsy, and mental retardation as well as with educational problems such as reading difficulties, and school failure generally. However, the correlation between impulsivity and IQ is small (.16 to .30 depending on the measure of impulsivity that is used). With regard to affective variables, impulsives are more aggressive, while reflectives are more attentive, more advanced in moral judgments, and more able to delay gratification. Impulsivity is also correlated with heart rate (.45) with impulsives having higher heart rates than reflectives.

Field independence is also related to a variety of personality characteristics (Witkin & Goodenough, 1977). Although identified with only simple perceptual tasks, field dependents show a greater use of social referents in ambiguous situations, while field independents are more autonomous. Field dependents are more attentive to social cues, have an interpersonal orientation, are emotionally open, and gravitate toward social situations. Field independents, on the other hand, have an impersonal orientation, remain distant from others both physically and psychologically, and prefer non-social situations.

Intellectually, field independents may have somewhat higher IQs but their particular strength is in spatial abilities (Kogan, 1976). This is not surprising since the rod and frame task and the embedded figures task used to measure field independence require spatial judgments. In fact, the correlation between field independence and spatial ability (about .43) is further supported by a correlation of .32 between field independence and a measure of right hemisphere advantage (i.e. a dichotic listening task scored for the left ear) (Bloom-Feshback, 1980). It appears that field independents have an advantage in the right hemisphere and the associated spatial abilities and no advantage or disadvantage in the left hemisphere and associated verbal abilities.

Reviews of the major cognitive style variables (Kagan, 1976; Kogan, 1971) show a fairly consistent picture of the style. The links between cognitive styles and personality are abundant with the different style variables distinguishing primarily between overcontrol (rigidity, field independence, reflection, analytic, narrow categorization, categorical style) at one extreme and undercontrol (flexibility, field dependence, impulsivity, global, broad categorization, descriptive style) at the other. The people at the overcontrolled extreme are object oriented and those at the undercontrolled extreme are people oriented, thus suggesting a relationship with the personality variable, extraversion-introversion (Guilford, 1980).

In fact, comparing descriptions and treatment implications of cognitive style variables (e.g. Witkin, Moore, Goodenough & Cox, 1977) and of extraversion (Eysenck, 1967; Wakefield, 1979) and psychoticism (Eysenck & Eysenck, 1977) shows reasonable consistencies between the cognitive style and personality variables. The following educational implications (from Witkin, et al., 1977) apply equally well to different cognitive styles or to differences in the extraversion variable. Field dependents (and extraverts) are more attentive and have better memory for social material. They are more reliant on external references, goals, and reinforcements, and (along with subjects high on psychoticism) are less likely to use analyzing, structuring, abstracting, or general principles on their own. While there is little research correlating cognitive style measures and personality questionnaires directly, what there is (Evans, 1971; Forrest, 1971; Eysenck & Eysenck, 1971, Eysenck & Eysenck, 1977) suggests that cognitive styles correlate highly with extraversion-introversion as well as with psychoticism, and to a lesser extent neuroticism.

The relations between cognitive style and IQ are usually small (Kogan, 1976) although cognitive styles and spatial ability are substantially related (Bloom-Feshback, 1980). The link between cognitive style and extraversion and the link between cognitive style and spatial ability are particularly interesting in light of the evidence (Riding & Dyer, 1980) that extraversion and ability differences are directly related. Extraverted children have higher verbal than spatial abilities, and introverted children have higher spatial than verbal abilities. Although the relationships are not perfect, they suggest that these three sets of variables influence each other. A possible system of causal relationships among these variables is that a child's stronger ability (spatial or verbal) during development pushes the child to become more oriented to information from objects or from people. The spatially strong, object oriented, child develops the effective scanning strategies, analytical skills, reflection, and independence associated with the overcontrolled cognitive styles and an introverted personality. The spatially weak child develops an extraverted personality from attaining most information from other people, but is less effective with scanning and analytical skills and is more dependent and impulsive in his (undercontrolled) cognitive style.

MEASUREMENT OF COGNITIVE STYLES

The two major cognitive style variables are measured by visual perceptual tasks. Field independence is measured by either the rod and frame test, the embedded figures test, or (less frequently) the body adjustment test (Witkin, et al., 1962). The rod and frame test involves adjusting a luminous rod to the vertical position in a dark room while misleading cues are given with a luminous frame surrounding the rod. The score is the number of degrees that the rod deviates from the vertical. The body adjustment test is similar but requires the subject to adjust his or her own body to the vertical position. The embedded figures test requires the subject to identify geometric figures embedded within other figures. All three tests are highly correlated and have forms that can be administered to children as young as five years (Kogan, 1976) as well as to adults.

Reflection-impulsivity is measured by the *Matching Familiar Figures Test* (MFFT) which has forms appropriate for preschoolers, school-aged children, and adults (Messer, 1975). An item on the MFFT consists of a drawing of, say, a bear and several similar drawings below it. Only one of these drawings is exactly like the one at the top, and the subject's task is to identify it. The test is scored for both the time it takes the subject to give the first response to each item (fast times are impulsive; slow are reflective) and the number of errors the subject makes (accuracy). Reflectives are the subjects who are slow to respond and accurate. Impulsives are those who respond quickly and inaccurately. Although errors and response times are correlated, there is a substantial number of fast-accurate responders and slow-inaccurate responders who are usually not considered either impulsive or reflective, but simply high and low ability, respectively (Kogan, 1976).

Other cognitive styles are also typically measured with visual (or occasionally auditory or kinesthetic) perceptual tasks. The requirements of the tasks are different for the different variables (Guilford, 1980). Several, such as conceptual style and equivalence range, require the subject to classify a set of stimuli into subsets. Leveling versus sharpening requires that figures be reproduced from memory. Levelers smooth over irregularities, and sharpeners exaggerate them. Focusing versus scanning is measured by whether the subject focuses his or her attention on specific aspects of the stimulus or scans for additional information.

CAUSES OF INDIVIDUAL DIFFERENCES IN COGNITIVE STYLES

Surprisingly little work has been done to investigate the causes of individual differences in cognitive styles. In most of the early work, it was assumed that cognitive styles had a genetic or physiological basis but this point was not emphasized (Wardell & Royce, 1978). Cognitive styles such as sharpening versus leveling were heavily influenced by Gestalt Psychology which assumes genetic causes of perception. Reflection-impulsivity was initially influenced by concerns over the negative effects of impulsivity on school performance. The impulsive behavior of children with minimal brain dysfunction, a presumably constitutional condition, has inspired many of the attempts to apply the research on impulsivity to practical settings.

Recent work (e.g. Karoly & Briggs, 1978; Karp, 1963) has been concerned with manipulating cognitive styles experimentally. Typically, attempts are made to make an impulsive child more reflective or help a field dependent person "overcome" this condition. In the case of reflection-impulsivity, some manipulation is possible, especially when a rationale for not responding impulsively is presented to the child. Experimental manipulation of cognitive styles demonstrates some environmental influence on them, but the effects appear not to be large and long-term follow-ups have not been reported. Since cognitive style variables appear to be relatively stable over time (Kogan, 1976) and show large differences within school classes taught in a more or less standard fashion, non-environmental factors should be suspected of influencing them.

Most theoretical statements concerning the causes of cognitive style variables have dealt with either personality (Kagan & Kogan, 1970), abilities (Guilford, 1980), or both (Wardell & Royce, 1978) as causes of variations in cognitive styles. Also it is possible that cognitive style measures are simply different ways to measure personality or abilities and are not something else that is "caused" by personality or abilities. To the extent that cognitive styles are caused by or are the same as either personality or abilities, the causes of these variables are also the causes of cognitive styles.

Spatial ability is heavily involved in cognitive styles (Bloom-Feshback, 1980) and shares its right hemisphere physiology basis with cognitive styles (or at least with field independence). The visual perceptual nature of the measures that are used for all the cognitive style variables and the correlations among these measures suggest that spatial ability underlies all cognitive style variables. Spatial ability itself has been shown to be highly heritable (McGee, 1979), and these hereditary factors certainly influence cognitive styles by way of spatial ability.

All major personality variables are associated with cognitive style variables as discussed earlier. Field independence-dependence is clearly linked to introversion-extraversion. Anxiety and psychoticism as well as extraversion are related to reflection-impulsivity. Once again, the correlations among the various cognitive style variables suggest that these personality variables underly all of them. We have also seen that these personality variables are moderately heritable. These hereditary factors influence cognitive styles by way of the personality variables. Demonstrations that personality variables and ability variables are themselves related (Riding & Dyer, 1980) suggest that common hereditary factors influence personality and abilities and that these common hereditary factors in personality and abilities result in differences in cognitive style.

CONSEQUENCES OF COGNITIVE STYLES

The consequences of differences in cognitive styles follow in a straightforward fashion once it is seen that cognitive style variables typically distinguish between an overcontrolled, object-oriented style (field independent, reflective, etc.) and an undercontrolled, people-oriented style (field dependent, impulsive, etc.). The object-oriented group behaves in the same manner as introverts (in fact, they are introverts), and the people-oriented group has the same behavior as extraverts (they are extraverts). Interpersonally, field dependents and impulsives seek people, get information from people, and appear to enjoy their company. Field independents and reflectives are distant from other people, get information from non-social stimuli (objects), and are relatively indifferent to the company of others (Witkin & Goodenough, 1977; Messer, 1976).

Vocational preferences of field independents and field dependents also follow from their object versus people orientations (Witkin, 1976). Field independents (object-oriented) prefer natural sciences, engineering, and mathematics. Field dependents (people-oriented) prefer jobs in the social sciences. These preferences are similar to the preferences of introverts and extraverts (Holder & Wankowski, 1980). Even with a single occupation, field dependents and field independents perform differently. Teachers—an occupation that has been widely studied with respect to cognitive styles—who are field independent are concerned with the cognitive aspects of learning and tend to present information systematically, often in lecture form. Teachers who are field dependent are warmer, more interested in their students personally, and use class discussions more (Witkin, et al., 1977).

The educational consequences of differences in cognitive styles are also pronounced. Field independents are at an advantage with individual work requiring them to analyze or use general principles with non-social material. Field dependents, on the other hand have better memory for social material and may be at an advantage when working with others and when external goals or rewards are available (Witkin, et al., 1977). Teachers' tendencies to use methods consistent with their own cognitive styles affect the learning of their students. Students learn better with teachers of the same cognitive style as their own (Packer & Bain, 1978).

While the research on field independence has typically been balanced, showing different advantages for both field independents and field dependents, the research on reflection-impulsivity has been more one-sided. Reflection is usually associated with success and impulsivity with failure (Messer, 1976). Recently some evidence has become available indicating that success in school is associated with intermediate levels of reflection-impulsivity, rather than with the most reflective style (Fraioli, 1978; Testo, 1979). Apparently a student can be too reflective for optimal learning, as well as too impulsive.

USES OF COGNITIVE STYLE VARIABLES

Cognitive style variables may be used in educational and vocational counseling settings to match a person's cognitive strategies with the demands of the task. There are three ways to assure that an appropriate match is made—assignment, manipulation of the person's cognitive style, and modification of the demands of the task.

In educational settings, the most convenient way of using cognitive style information is usually by assignment. Since students learn best with teachers of similar cognitive styles, a student can be assigned to a teacher of similar cognitive style. If this is impractical the teacher can use techniques (lectures or discussions, group or individual work) appropriate to the student's cognitive style even though these techniques are not the ones generally preferred by the teacher. In cases where the mismatch between the task and the student is small, the teacher may attempt to change the student's style slightly. Particularly if the student is slightly (not dramatically) too impulsive, the teacher may explain the importance of careful responding and reward longer response times. If the mismatch between the task and the student's cognitive style is large it may be more productive to consider changing the demands of the task to fit the student. There is usually more than one way to learn or perform a task.

In vocational counseling, cognitive style variables may be helpful in advising a person concerning appropriate and inappropriate jobs. This is basically the same as assignment, but the final decision is left with the person being advised. Often specific advice based on the person's cognitive style will be unnecessary since the individual will already express interests consistent with cognitive style. In cases where a person's stated vocational goals are inconsistent with cognitive style—because of family pressure, the prestige, or the monetary rewards of a particular job—information about cognitive style can be helpful in resolving the conflict. If the mismatch is small and the other considerations are very important, the person might be encouraged to modify his or her style in the appropriate direction. If the mismatch is large, alternate vocations that are more aligned with personal cognitive style and that yield similar rewards can be explored.

Although cognitive styles are not explicitly used for selection in educational or industrial settings, the widespread use of ability tests and personality questionnaires, which are both related to cognitive styles, assures that cognitive styles affect selection decisions.

Diagnostic uses of cognitive style variables are also limited. Impulsivity is a concern with hyperactive, brain damaged, retarded, and epileptic persons, and measures of impulsivity are used, along with a wide variety of other information, with these people. Other variables such as scanning versus focusing and breadth of conceptualization may be used occasionally to clarify perceptual and intellectual problems.

SUMMARY

Individual differences in cognitive styles have been discussed. Cognitive styles include field independence-dependence, reflection-impulsivity and several other similar variables. These variables are usually measured by tests involving perceptual tasks. Different cognitive style measures are positively correlated among themselves and measure a dimension running from overcontrolled object-oriented styles at one extreme to undercontrolled, people-oriented styles at the other. Spatial abilities and several personality variables are related to and possibly cause differences in cognitive styles. Differences in cognitive styles influence educational, vocational, and interpersonal behavior and can be used practically for matching a person's preferred cognitive style with the demands of specific tasks.

CHAPTER 8

VOCATIONAL INTERESTS

Assessing vocational interests to allow people to seek and prepare for jobs that should be satisfying for them and in which they should be productive has been a concern for psychologists since the late 1800s, although practical measures were not developed until after World War I (Crites, 1969). For several decades, psychologists were involved in programs designed to match individuals to jobs based on their abilities and interests and the characteristics of the jobs and the people with whom employees in these jobs would be working.

It was recognized that people with different characteristics were attracted to different jobs. One such characteristic, but certainly not the only one, is intelligence. Some jobs make greater intellectual demands on a worker than do other jobs. The jobs requiring greater skills usually require an extended period of training prior to beginning work. Since intelligence is highly related to successful completion of most educational and training programs, the jobs requiring extended training are only open to those with high intelligence. Jobs requiring shorter (or less intense) training are open to people with lower intelligence as well as to people with high intelligence who choose to work in these jobs.

The term level is used to describe the constellation of responsibility, capacity, and skill (Roe, 1956). The level of an occupation also refers to the level of education needed to pursue the occupation. In practical work, the level of education required by an occupation is the most important meaning of the term level.

Jobs requiring different levels of education and intelligence vary in other characteristics as well. Those requiring higher levels of intelligence are generally more prestigious (lawyer, physician) than those requiring moderate intelligence (policeman, nurse) which are in turn more prestigious than those requiring very little intelligence (unskilled workers) (Canter, 1956). In addition to prestige, the incomes of the jobs generally correspond with their intellectual requirements, although not perfectly. Although the prestige, income, and intellectual demands of most jobs are either all high (e.g., physicians), all moderate (skilled workers), or all low (unskilled workers), there are several occupations that have relatively high prestige and intellectual demands but lower income, such as teachers, clergy, and nurses. These occupations have traditions of unselfish (or some may say unrealistic) service to others. Other occupations with less prestige and lower intellectual requirements yield higher incomes than would be expected because of effective unions, favorable licensing laws, or artificially low numbers admitted to pursue the occupation.

In addition to level, occupations are distinguished by fields. Fields are different types of jobs that are not primarily associated with different overall intellectual requirements, although some fields are at slightly higher levels than others. Fields are distinguished by their requirements for different specific abilities and interests. For example, a person with high spatial and mechanical abilities might choose engineering, while another person with high verbal skills might become a writer or English teacher. In the area of interests, a person who likes to work with people might be attracted to teaching English or teaching engineering while another person less interested in working with people might prefer the similar, but less social, jobs of writing or drafting (e.g. Knapp & Knapp, 1981).

The first practical measure of vocational interests was developed in 1927 by Strong (Layton, 1960). Although Strong was concerned with matching men and jobs, the measurement of job characteristics had not been developed. Consequently, he adopted the strategy of matching the interests of people considering various occupations with the interests of people already successfully pursuing those occupations. Presumably these people had managed to match themselves with their jobs reasonably well without benefit of an interest questionnaire, and other people like them could also be expected to match the requirements of the various occupations. *The Strong Vocational Interest Blank* resulted and has been widely used since. (The current version is called the *Strong-Campbell Interest Inventory*). This questionnaire requires that the subject respond in terms of like or dislike for the various items on the questionnaire. The subject's interests are scored for similarity to the interests of persons in a large number of occupations. A high score on an occupational scale (e.g. mathematicians) indicates that the subject's interests are similar to those of mathematicians, and a low score indicates that these interests are not similar to those of mathematicians. Typically, a subject's interests will match the interest of workers in several fields reasonably well.

Strong's approach involved measuring the interests of a person and matching these interests to each of a large number of jobs separately. It soon became apparent that the interests of people in several occupations were very similar. This is particularly true of jobs that are very similar. For example, air conditioner repairmen and refrigerator repairmen share interests and abilities that attract them to their jobs and insure success, although the specific techniques they must learn to perform their jobs vary somewhat. On the other hand, some jobs are associated with quite different patterns of interests. For instance, the interests of repairmen are very different from those of social workers or ministers.

Several attempts have been made to identify general interest traits that distinguish among occupations. The best known and probably the strongest of these is the distinction between interest in things versus interest in people (Crites, 1969). Occupations such as retail sales or receptionist are generally filled with people who like to interact with other people. The opportunity to work with others attracts them to these jobs, and their continued interest and ability to interact with people is related to their success at their job. Other jobs, such as truck driving or mechanics, are filled with people who are more interested in things than in people. They prefer to interact with machines. This distinction between working with things and working with people is reminiscent of the vocational preferences of introverts (things) and extraverts (people) (Holder & Wankowski, 1980) and the corresponding preferences of persons with different cognitive styles (Witkin, 1976) that were discussed previously. The similarity between vocational interests and personality has been widely researched (Crites, 1969; Dunteman & Bailey, 1967; Wakefield & Cunningham, 1975; Ward, Cunningham, & Wakefield, 1976; Walsh, 1974). The relationship between interests and cognitive styles has also been considered, although far less often (Osipow, 1969).

Other interest traits that distinguish among occupations have been identified. Clerical versus mechanical interests have been found to distinguish between two groups of jobs (Clark & Campbell, 1965). Persons performing various "clerical" jobs, such as sales clerk, stock clerk and printer, were similar on this trait. Persons performing "mechanical" jobs, such as truck driver, sheet metal worker, and plumber, were similar among themselves but opposite to the "clerical" group on this trait. Super and Crites (1962) suggest the following dimensions of vocational interests: scientific, social-welfare, literary, material, systematic, contact and aesthetic. Each of these dimensions distinguishes workers in one group of occupations from workers in other groups of occupations.

Since some occupations are associated with similar interests, efforts to group occupations into useful, categories began early (Roe, 1956). It makes no sense to use interest scores to help decide which of two jobs to seek if the interests associated with the jobs are almost identical. On the other hand, interests can be very effective for distinguishing between jobs associated with dissimilar interests. The problem was to identify groups of jobs associated with similar interests within the groups but dissimilar interest between them. Interest questionnaires can then be used effectively to help a person decide which of the several groups of occupations for which the individual might be best fitted while other information (e.g. abilities, required training, availability of jobs) must be used to decide among the jobs within a group.

Roe's (1956) theory of occupations consists of a circular arrangement of eight interest groups based on earlier factor analytic work (e.g. Guilford,

Christensen, Bond & Sutton, 1954) and a series of six levels representing responsibility, capacity, and skill within each of the groups. The order of the groups around the circle indicates the similarity of the interests to each other. The order of interests is service, business contact organization, technology, outdoor, science, general, cultural, arts and entertainment, and back to service. Each of these groups is further divided into six levels: professional and managerial 1, professional and managerial 2, semi-professional and small business, skilled, semi-skilled, and unskilled. At the higher levels, the eight groups are more distinct, while at the lowest level (unskilled) the eight interest groups are all relatively similar (Roe & Klos, 1969).

Following Roe's (1956) theory of occupations, Knapp and Knapp (1981) have presented a practical questionnaire, the *California Occupational Preference System* (COPSystem), for measuring the eight interest groups. The six levels of Roe's theory are reduced to the professional level and the skilled level to reflect practical concern about whether a person needs advanced professional training to pursue his vocational interests or whether shorter, less expensive training will suffice. At levels lower than the skilled level, distinctions among the eight interest groups are relatively small and thus not measured.

Figure 8.1
Roe's Eight Vocational Groups (from Knapp & Knapp, 1981)

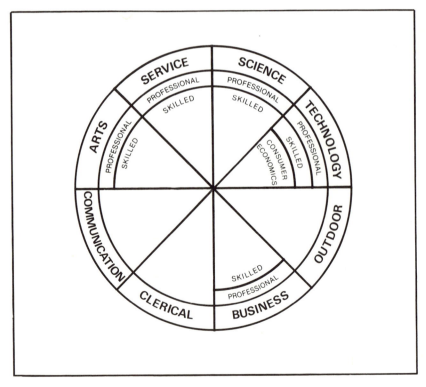

A similar set of occupational groups inspired by Roe's theory is Holland's (1973) set of six occupational types. The first is called Realistic and includes most outdoor and mechanical jobs, such as forest ranger and airplane mechanic which are separate groups in Roe's theory. The second type is Investigative and includes occupations of a scientific nature such as chemist or biologist. The Artistic group of occupations is self-explanatory. Next is Social which includes teaching, counseling, social work and similar occupations. The Enterprising occupations include sales jobs and other occupations involving convincing and leading others (lawyers, politicians). The sixth group is called Conventional and includes clerical and routine jobs such as accountants, secretaries, and computer operators.

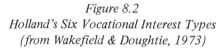

Figure 8.2
Holland's Six Vocational Interest Types
(from Wakefield & Doughtie, 1973)

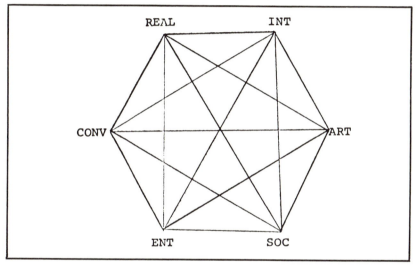

Holland has constructed interest questionnaires (Holland, 1965; Holland, 1972) designed to classify people into the same six types. Based on their responses, people can be grouped into those having realistic, investigative, artistic, social, enterprising, or conventional interests. Of course, most people have some interests in more than one area, and their second and third areas of interest are also identified and used for vocational counseling. A person's highest level of interest might be in, say, the social area with nearly as high interests in the enterprising and artistic areas. This person might look for a job in any of these areas (avoiding the other areas) or plan a career incorporating all of them. For example, this person might train to be a music teacher (both artistic and social) and strive to become an educational administrator or an officer in a professional association (enterprising). Of course, many other career plans consistent with his interests could be made depending on his abilities, previous training, and the job market.

A person whose interests are all (or mostly) in one (or a few) areas is said to have homogeneous interests. Homogeneous persons have patterns of very high and very low scores on interest questionnaires. Heterogeneous interests are shown by a pattern of similar levels of interest in most areas. Persons with well developed homogeneous interests are likely to have more stable vocational choices, greater academic and vocational achievement, and greater job satisfaction (Holland, 1966; Holland & Holland, 1977).

A person's choice of vocation may be congruent or incongruent with his or her pattern of interests. Although most choices are congruent with, for example, persons with investigative interests pursuing investigative occupations (O'Neil, Magoon, & Tracy, 1978), incongruent choices often occur. For these people, there is a mismatch between their measured interests and the interests associated with their occupations. In general, persons whose interests and occupations are congruent, are more stable, achieve more, and are more satisfied with their jobs than are persons with incongruent interests and occupations (Holland, 1966; Spokane, 1979).

Another feature of Holland's theory is the interrelations among the six types. Their interrelationships are represented by a hexagon with each type placed on one corner. The order of types around the hexagon is Realistic, Investigative, Artistic, Social, Enterprising, Conventional, and back to Realistic. The distance between each two types represents their similarity. For example, the Realistic type is similar to (although clearly distinguishable from) the Investigative type on one side and the Conventional type on the other. It is less similar to the Artistic and Enterprising types that are farther away and very dissimilar from the Social type which is opposite to Realistic in the hexagon. The similarity (or dissimilarity) of any two types can be obtained by considering their relative placements in the hexagon.

The hexagonal arrangement of the six vocational and interest types has received a great deal of support (Wakefield & Doughtie, 1973; Osipow, Ashby, and Wall, 1966). The hexagonal arrangement of interests occurs in different racial groups (Wakefield, Yom, Doughtie, Chang, & Alston, 1975), in both sexes (Alston, et al., 1976), and with different measuring instruments (Cole, 1973; Bobele, et al., 1975). The hexagonal arrangement is also valid for identifiable subgroups of persons for whom vocational counseling could be valuable (Cunningham, et al., 1977). The generality of the interrelationships among vocational interests has resulted in their being included not only on Holland's questionnaires but on the most recent revision of Strong's pioneering questionnaire, now called the *Strong-Campbell Interest Inventory.*

By considering the interrelations among the six types, the consistency of a person's interests can be determined (Holland, 1966; Walsh, 1974). Persons whose interests are in similar areas are said to be consistent, while those whose interests are in dissimilar areas are inconsistent. Consistent interests lead to greater stability, achievement, and satisfaction than dissimilar interests. For example, persons whose interests are in the consistent Conventional and Realistic areas and choose an occupation that is congruent with one or both areas, such as computer operator, would probably be happier with their jobs and work at them longer and more diligently than would persons with inconsistent Conventional and Artistic interests. When a person's interests are in inconsistent areas, it is very difficult to find a job that is congruent with all interests.

Grouping occupations together based on their similarities has been successful for both Roe's (1956) and Holland's (1973) similar sets of groups. The alternative is considering each job separately even though many jobs attract workers with very similar interests and abilities. It is pointless to try to distinguish between very similar jobs such as social worker and marriage counselor based on interests or abilities. The interests and abilities required for both jobs are extremely similar, although the training in specific skills and information used in the jobs are somewhat different. On the other hand, distinguishing between these occupations, both of which are Social, and occupations such as accounting and bookkeeping, both of which are Conventional, is quite easy using an interest questionnaire. A recent review of personnel selection (Pearlman, 1980) concludes that job families (i.e. groups of similar jobs) based on human attribute requirements (i.e. individual differences in interests and abilities) or on the broad content of the jobs are more promising for both theory and application than molecular analysis of each job.

CORRELATES OF VOCATIONAL INTERESTS

Two areas of individual differences must be considered in relation to vocational interests—personality and aptitudes. The relationship between personality and interest is important because theories of interest often use personality as an explanatory concept, with interests either being identical to personality or arising from the interaction of personality and environment (Roe, 1956; Holland, 1973). The relationship between vocational interests and vocational aptitudes (or abilities) is important because the two can be very easily confused. Interests refer to what a person likes and dislikes while aptitudes refer to the ability to perform various jobs.

The relationship between interest and personality questionnaires has been widely investigated as a result of the close theoretical correspondence between them and the similarity between the two kinds of questionnaire. The relationship between personality as measured by the *Minnesota Multiphasic Personality Inventory* (MMPI) and interest measured by the *Strong Vocational Interest Blank* (SVIB) is substantial (Dunteman & Bailey, 1967). The personality factor with the strongest relationship to vocational interests is introversion-extraversion distinguishing between interests in occupations such as author (introverted) and social worker (extraverted). Since the MMPI is primarily a measure of abnormality, it is not surprising that an abnormal factor also distinguished among interests. Although not as strong as the introversion-extraversion distinction, there was a tendency for high scores on psychotic scales (schizophrenia and psychopathic deviate) to be associated with utilitarian interests and for high scores on neurotic scales (depression, hypochondriasis) to be associated with social service interests. This pattern is very similar to the pattern of college majors chosen by persons with different personality scores (Holder & Wankowski, 1980).

Similarly, theoretically consistent relationships occur between interests measured by the *Vocational Preference Inventory* (VPI) and personality measured by the *Sixteen Personality Factors Questionnaire* (16PF) (Ward, Cunningham, & Wakefield, 1976). Artistic and enterprising interests are associated with tender-minded and imaginative personality characteristics. Enterprising interests were also related to assertive, conservative, and venturesome personality characteristics, while Conventional interests were associated with humble and shy personalities. The 16PF is widely used in vocational counseling and the personality scores of workers in a large number of occupations have been compiled (Cattell & Eber, & Tatsuoka, 1970).

A personality measure of needs, the *Edwards Personal Preference Schedule* (EPPS), also is related to vocational interests (Wakefield & Cunningham, 1975). Investigative and Artistic interests are associated with high need for change and low needs for order and abasement, while Conventional interests (opposite to artistic in Holland's theory) are associated with exactly the opposite pattern of needs. Investigative interests are also associated with high needs for achievement, succorance, and endurance and low needs for intraception and nurturance. Enterprising interests are associated with low needs for intraception and nurturance.

Within the personality domain, values or feelings about the worth of an activity may be distinguished from interests in the activity. In comparisons of questionnaires designed to measure values and questionnaires designed to measure interests, significant relationships are obtained between the value attached to an area of activity and the degree of interest expressed in it (Knapp & Knapp, 1979). In fact these relationships can be quite large when sophisticated statistical procedures are applied (Thorndike, Weiss & Dawis, 1968). However, these relationships may be artificially inflated by the similarity of the questions used on value and interest inventories (Katz, 1969). Although the relationships between values and interests support the association of personality and interests, the relationships are low enough that separate measures of interests and values, as well as personality, must be administered in practical work (Knapp & Knapp, 1980).

Correlations between interests and aptitudes are mostly low (about .20) (Crites, 1969). These correlations indicate that a person may be very interested in a particular job but not have the abilities necessary to perform it well. Another person may be able to perform the job well but dislike it. These low correlations do indicate a slight tendency for interests and aptitudes to be consistent, but for practical purposes it would be a severe error to interpret a person's interests in particular activities as indicating that the person would probably be "able" to do them well. Separate ability tests must be administered for this purpose (L. Knapp & R. Knapp, 1981).

On the other hand, when one person's interests are ordered from highest to lowest and aptitudes are similarly ordered, the relationship between interests and aptitude within the person is usually higher (in the .40s) (Wesley, Corey & Stewart, 1950). This means that a person's high interest areas usually correspond with highest abilities. However, if all his abilities are low in comparison to other people he may not be "able" to compete with them even in the highest ability (and interest) area. Similarly, a person with generally high abilities may develop a distaste for activities recognized as requiring abilities that are not quite as high as other abilities. Even though dislike (low interest) is stated for those activities, such an individual is likely to perform them well compared to other people. It appears that a person's interests are highly related to abilities as they are perceived.

MEASUREMENT OF VOCATIONAL INTERESTS

Widely used measures of vocational interests are the *Strong-Campbell Interest Inventory* (SCII) (Campbell, 1977), which is the revised form of the *Strong Vocational Interest Blank* (SVIB) (Strong, 1943), Holland's questionnaires, the *Vocational Preference Inventory* (VPI) (Holland, 1965) and the *Self-Directed Search* (SDS) (Holland, 1972), and the *California Occupational Preference System* (COPS) (Knapp & Knapp, 1981), which can be used with companion measures of values (Knapp & Knapp, 1980) and abilities (L. Knapp & R. Knapp, 1981). All of these interest questionnaires contain items to which the subject must respond by marking personal likes or dislikes for the activities or jobs mentioned.

Strong's questionnaires, the SVIB and the SCII, contain large numbers of scales corresponding to different occupations, such as attorney, physician, and accountant. Each of these scales was developed by contrasting the responses of members of a specific occupation to the response of "men-in-general." Items that distinguish an occupation from the general sample are scored on the scale for that occupation. A subject's responses are scored for all occupations, and the similarity between the individual's interests and those of members of each occupation is given a letter score—A for high similarity, B+, B, B- for less similarity, and C for low similarity. The high similarity scores indicate occupations pursued by people with interests similar to those of the subject and in which the subject would presumably fit well. The SCII has six general scales corresponding to Holland's six categories.

Holland's VPI and SDS ask the subject to respond directly to lists of jobs, indicating his liking or disliking for each. The items are scored for the six categories discussed previously, and the subject's general interest scores are used in conjunction with a long list of jobs and their interest profiles to explore a wide range of possible jobs about which the subject might not know. From these possibilities, realistic options are chosen. The SDS includes, in addition to a list of jobs, lists of activities, perceived competencies, and self-ratings that are all independently scored for the six categories. This procedure gives a broader sample of information as well as allowing the possibility of uncovering inconsistencies between the subject's interest in a job title and disinterest in the activities involved in the job.

The most comprehensive package available for vocational assessment is the series developed by Knapp and Knapp. The interest inventory, the COPS, consists of 168 job activity descriptions to which the examinee indicates liking or disliking of each activity. These items are scored into 14 interest clusters derived from Roe's (1956) theory of eight groups and six levels. Each of the eight interest groups is represented. A distinction between the professional level and the skilled level is made for most of the groups. This inventory is the vocational interest inventory that has been most directly influenced by factor analytic work on vocational interests. It can be used with the factor analytically constructed *Career Orientation Placement and Evaluation System* (COPES) to measure work values and the *Career Ability Placement Survey* (CAPS) to measure abilities. The three questionnaires together represent a far more complete vocational assessment than may be obtained with any other single series of measures.

CAUSES OF VOCATIONAL INTERESTS

Vocational interests develop in a fairly regular pattern. The child sees other adults (especially parents) at work or hears them talk about work. The child may develop interests consistent with the parent's interests or the interests of other important adults in the environment. These interests are encouraged or discouraged by parents, teachers, and peers. Information is received concerning the relative prestige and incomes of various occupations from numerous sources. All this information results in vocational aspirations that are often not very realistic but become more realistic as the child grows up (Holland, 1973). Early vocational interests of children include such unrealistic (for most people) occupations as cowboy or spaceman that are likely to be taken from television.

As the child reaches the teenage years, these choices become less frequent and are replaced by choices that actually occur in the child's environment. The stated aspirations at this age are still unrealistic for large numbers of teenagers. A far larger percentage of them choose highly prestigious occupations, such as doctors or lawyers, than can possibly enter these occupations (Gottfredson, 1979). During their late teens and early twenties, as they actually enter the job market or professional training, their aspirations come to match the available jobs.

Looking back from adulthood, the early vocational choices of the children with higher intelligence will be seen to have been more realistic than the choices of other children (Crites, 1969). Large numbers of children aspire to occupations that are very difficult to enter. The more able children actually do enter them and appear to have made an early realistic vocational choice, while other children will be forced to alter their decisions resulting in later realistic choices.

Vocational interests are usually thought to result in part from environmental influences. Certainly, they are influenced by the jobs that are available (Gottfredson, 1979). Most people do not retain aspirations that they cannot achieve, but adapt their aspirations to their actual circumstances. Also, the early unrealistic vocational interests of children obviously come from television and movies. Another piece of evidence that is usually interpreted as an environmental influence is the correspondence between vocational interests of parents and those of their children, although this correspondence could result from either the environmental or the genetic similarity of parents and children. Recent studies (e.g., Schneider, DeWinne, & Overton, 1980) indicate that parental occupation interests (especially those of the father) are related with their children's vocational interests (especially their daughters'). It should be noted that the correspondence between parents' and children's vocational interests is not exact, as would result in lawyers' children becoming the next generation of lawyers, but their levels and general areas of occupations are related (Crites, 1969).

While there has been little recent concern with the possibility that vocational interests may have genetic causes, at least one older study (Carter, 1932) dealt with that possibility. In that study, monozygotic twins, who are genetically identical, had much more similar vocational interests than dizygotic twins, who are less genetically similar but still share the same environments. Findings such as this support the idea that interests are influenced genetically. Also, the interests of like-sex and different sex dizygotic twins showed about the same relationship, indicating that being treated as a boy or as a girl did little to lower the relationship between the vocational interests of twins. The extra genetic similarity of monozygotic twins was far more effective in making the vocational interests of twins similar.

In a recent large study primarily concerned with ability and personality traits, Osborne (1980) cites unpublished evidence by Breland (1972) that monozygotic twins are more similar than dizygotic twins on interest variables as well as on personality and ability variables. This evidence supports the idea (Allen, 1970) that all psychological traits (including interests) are about equally heritable and that the heritabilities of these traits are moderate (rather than extremely high or extremely low). The interests considered in this study were the practical, science, business, clerical, helping, and artistic interests measured by the *Strong Vocational Interest Blank*.

A further indication of genetic effects is a recent comparison of German men named Smith (Schmied or Schmid in German) and Tailor (Schneider in German) (Baumler, 1980). Men with these names are presumably descended from smiths and tailors who took the names of their occupations as their surnames. On questionnaires administered to those two groups, the Smiths saw themselves as less suitable for professions involving agility and more suitable for professions and sports involving strength than the Tailors saw themselves. In addition, the Smiths were taller, heavier, and more solid than the Tailors and had a greater preference for hobbies involving strength. These findings are consistent with possible genetic effects coming from the time when stronger smiths and more agile tailors took their names from their occupations.

Indirect evidence of genetic influence on vocational interests is given by their correlations with personality variables which are moderately genetically determined (Eaves, 1973). Particularly the extraversion-introversion personality dimension and the pervasive vocational distinction between interest in people and interest in things are related. It is very likely that the people versus things interest dimension is simply the heritable extraversion-introversion dimension measured in a vocational context. Also, the relationship between the highly heritable general intelligence factor and occupational level (Canter, 1956) strongly suggests a genetic influence on a person's actual occupation, if not on his vocational interests as such. A similar effect of mathematics ability on choice of college major, and thus occupation, has been presented (Goldman & Hewitt, 1976). Mathematics ability with heritable components such as spatial ability (McGee, 1979), predicts whether a student will choose a science major (high math) or a non-science major (low math), although once the choice has been made, verbal ability predicts success in all majors better than math does.

Genetic effects on vocational interests and vocational choices must operate on broad differences between occupations rather than on specific choices. A person may be disposed to work with people in an intellectual way rather than perform isolated work with machines based on heritable personality and ability traits. However, specific choices, such as whether to study, and consequently to teach, either psychology or sociology, for example, must result from information, opportunities, and encouragement received from other people.

CONSEQUENCES OF VOCATIONAL INTERESTS

Like most psychological variables, vocational interests are measured to predict behaviors in the future. Just as intelligence tests were constructed to predict educational achievement, vocational interest questionnaires were constructed to predict which occupation a person would enter (Strong, 1943). Although occupational choice is affected by variables other than interests, such as the availability of jobs (Gottfredson, 1979) and abilities (Ghiselli, 1966), interests play a central role in predicting which general area of occupation a person chooses to pursue as well as how satisfied, productive, and stable the person is in the job (Holland, 1973).

In fact, interest questionnaires predict occupational choice for long periods of time (Campbell, 1977; Holland, 1973). Interests, as compared to most other psychological variables, are remarkably stable over long periods of time. This allows substantial prediction of occupational choice years after a questionnaire is administered. Typically, interests predict the correct occupational area for over half of the people taking the questionnaire for periods as long as three and a half years (Spokane, 1979), seven years (O'Neil, Magoon and Tracey, 1978), and even 19 years (Zytowski, 1976). In addition, between 10 percent and 30 percent of the people taking interest questionnaires work in occupations that are similar to, but not exactly the same as, the ones they were predicted to pursue. Altogether, interest inventories predict occupations at least moderately well for up to 80 percent of the people who take them.

Since the educational preparation required for different occupations varies, it seems reasonable that vocational interests should predict which courses of study people follow. In fact, interest tests do predict courses of study reasonably well (Holland, 1973; Zytowski, 1976; O'Neil, Magoon & Tracey, 1978). They even predict which students are likely to change their college majors when they are not congruent with their interests (Holland, 1973). In fact, when students do change their major area of interest, they usually change to an area closely related to their original choice (Knapp, Knapp, and Buttafuoco, 1978). Interests also predict satisfaction for college students (Spokane, 1979) with those students whose interests and college majors are congruent reporting higher satisfaction.

Well developed vocational interests seem to motivate students to perform well in school. Students who report clear, consistent interests that are congruent with their fields of study are relatively successful. Students who have not developed clear vocational preferences, on the other hand, earn fewer credits, drop out of school more frequently, get lower grades, have higher anxiety, and become less involved (Holland & Holland, 1977). These students appear to lack the motivation to work hard at school because they are not working to achieve any goal, and they are not (usually) comfortable with their aimless studies. Of course, some of these students have simply had earlier career choices frustrated (by their low grades) and have undecided vocational interests as a result (rather than as a cause) of their academic failure. However, for practical purposes ability tests (L. Knapp & R. Knapp, 1981) rather than interest questionnaires should be used to predict school achievement.

Vocational interests also are related to students' study habits and attitudes (Wakefield, Alston, Yom, & Doughtie, 1974), although the question of whether the different interests actually cause the different study habits and attitudes is not resolved. Students with social and realistic (i.e. outdoor and mechanical) interests report that they approve of their teachers, but have limited acceptance of education generally and poor work methods. Probably these two groups of students have this pattern of study habits and attitudes for different reasons—the social students because they like people (including teachers) more than academics and the realistic students because they like jobs that do not generally require much academic preparation. On the other hand, conventional (i.e. clerical) and investigative students have good work methods and high educational acceptance, but relatively low teacher approval. This pattern of some interests being associated with high teacher approval and poor work methods and other interests being associated with low teacher approval and good work methods is suggestive of the effects of cognitive styles and personality on academic work. Field dependents and extraverts—and persons with social and realistic vocational interests—are more concerned with personal interaction with teachers and less conscientious about performing detailed work. In contrast, field independents and introverts—and persons with conventional and investigative vocational interests—are less concerned with teachers personally and more conscientious about detailed work.

USES OF VOCATIONAL INTERESTS

Measures of vocational interests are used primarily for vocational guidance. Along with measures of abilities, information about the availability of jobs and educational programs, and information about the person's financial assets and commitments, interest questionnaires can be used to explore the range of vocational possibilities and then to come to reasonable decisions. Exploration of new possibilities is at least as important a function of vocational interest questionnaires as is reaching decisions. It is unlikely that one person will be exposed sufficiently to a wide variety of occupations by the time he or she is expected to make a career choice in the teens or twenties. Often decisions made without considering a large number of alternatives are inadequate. Vocational interest questionnaires suggest a large number of possibilities while the person is filling in the questionnaire. After the questionnaire is scored for general areas of interest, extensive lists of jobs within his areas of interest (cf. Knapp & Knapp, 1981) suggest even more job possibilities that are closely related to the person's interests. Many of these may be jobs to which the individual has never been exposed and probably would not have considered without the use of a questionnaire.

Interest questionnaires are not generally used for the selection of personnel into specific jobs. These questionnaires, unlike ability tests, are easy to fake if the person taking them is given a reason. For example, a person applying for a job as a salesperson, is very likely to respond "yes" to a question asking about interest in sales even if the person really only wanted the job for the money.

Vocational interest questionnaires are more useful in situations involving assignment of people to various jobs, such as in the military or in organizations that are being reorganized but retaining the same personnel. When some job is assured, it is more likely that persons completing interest questionnaires will actually indicate which jobs would be most satisfying for them. Of course, even in assignment, interests cannot be used to make decisions in isolation from other information. Abilities, training, and the needs of the organization must also be considered.

A practical distinction that must be emphasized is the distinction between interest questionnaires and aptitude or ability tests. Interest questionnaires ask about a person's likes and dislikes, and although not completely unrelated to abilities, they are correctly interpreted only in terms of what a person will like or dislike. Frequently, persons who have taken an interest questionnaire and received high scores on some occupational scale, for instance, the scale for airline pilots, ask whether the scores mean they will be good airline pilots. This is a question of ability, not interest, and should be answered by an appropriate ability test (or tests), such as the *General Aptitude Test Battery* or the *Career Ability Placement Survey* (CAPS) (L. Knapp & R. Knapp, 1981), which predict capability to perform adequately in varous areas far better than any interest questionnaire possibly could (Knapp, Knapp & Michael, 1977; Knapp, Knapp, Strnad & Michael, 1978).

SUMMARY

Vocational interests and their measurement have been discussed. Interest questionnaires were developed for use in vocational guidance. Although they originally focused on specific jobs, most current interest questionnaires measure general areas of interest. Classification of jobs into general groups is a successful and widely used approach. Vocational interests are substantially related to personality variables and are related to a lesser extent with aptitudes (abilities). There is evidence of both environmental and genetic causes of vocational interests. Vocational interests influence a variety of occupational and educational variables in patterns reminiscent of the effects of personality and cognitive styles on these variables. Vocational interest questionnaires are primarily used for vocational guidance and assignment and should not be confused with aptitude or ability tests which may be used for selection.

REFERENCES

Allen, G. Within group and between group variation expected in human behavioral characteristics. *Behavior Genetics,* 1970, *1,* 175-194.

Alston, H. L. & Wakefield, J. A., Jr. Canonical analysis of the representational and automatic levels of the ITPA. *Psychology in the Schools,* 1974, *11,* 124-126.

Alston, H. L., Wakefield, J. A., Jr., Doughtie, E. B., & Bobele, R. M. Correspondence of constructs in Holland's theory for male and female college students. *Journal of Vocational Behavior,* 1976, *8,* 85-88.

Anastasi, A. *Psychological testing* (4th Ed.). New York: Macmillan, 1976.

Banta, T. J. Tests for the evaluation of early childhood education: The Cincinnati Autonomy Test Battery. In J. Hellmuth (Ed.), *Cognitive studies, Vol. 1.* New York: Brunner-Mazel, 1970.

Barron, F. *Creativity and psychological health.* Princeton, NJ: Van Nostrand, 1963.

Barron, F. *Creative person and creative process.* New York: Holt, Rinehart & Winston, 1969.

Baumler, G. Differences in physique in men called 'Smith' or 'Tailor' considered as results of a genetic effect dating back over several centuries. *Personality and Individual Differences,* 1980, *1,* 308-310.

Bennett, G. K., Seashore, H. G., & Wesman, A. G. *Counseling from profiles: A casebook for the Differential Aptitude Tests.* New York: Psychological Corporation, 1951.

Binet, A., & Simon, T. Methodes nouvelles pour le diagnostic du niveau intellectuel des anormaux. *Annee Psychologigue,* 1905, *11,* 191-244.

Bloom-Feshback, J. Differentiation: field dependence, spatial ability, and hemisphere specialization. *Journal of Personality,* 1980, *48,* 135-148.

Bobele, R. M., Alston, H. L., Wakefield, J. A., Jr., & Schnitzen, J. P. Relationships among Holland's personality types measured by an adjective checklist. *Journal of Vocational Behavior,* 1975, *7,* 201-206.

Bradley, P. E., Wakefield, J. A., Jr., Yom, B. L., Doughtie, E. B., Cox, J. A., & Kraft, I. A. Parental MMPIs and certain pathological behaviors in children. *Journal of Clinical Psychology,* 1974, *30,* 379-382.

Breland, N. S. A new approach to estimates of heritability from twin data. Unpublished research qualifying paper, Dept. of Educational Psychology, State University of New York at Buffalo, 1972.

Brody, E. B. & Brody, N. *Intelligence: Nature, determinants and consequences.* New York: Academic, 1976.

Broverman, D. M. Cognitive style and intraindividual variation in abilities. *Journal of Personality,* 1960, *28,* 240-256.

Campbell, D. P. *Manual, Strong Campbell Interest Inventory.* Palo Alto, CA: Stanford University Press, 1977.

Canter, R. R. Intelligence and the social status of occupations. *Personnel and Guidance Journal,* 1956, *34,* 258-260.

Carter, H. D. Twin similarities in occupational interests. *Journal of Educational Psychology,* 1932, *23,* 641-655.

Cattell, R. B., Eber, H. W., & Tatsuoka, M. M. *Handbook for the Sixteen Personality Factor Questionnaire (16PF).* Champaign, IL: Institute for Personality and Ability Testing, 1970.

Cattell, R. B., & Scheier, I. H. *The meaning and measurement of neuroticism and anxiety.* New York: Ronald Press, 1961.

Cole, N. S. On measuring the vocational interests of women. *Journal of Counseling Psychology,* 1973, *20,* 105-120.

Cooley, W. W., & Lohnes, P. R. *Multivariate data analysis.* New York: Wiley, 1971.

Cowden, J. E., Peterson, W. M., & Pacht, A. R. The validation of a brief screening test for verbal intelligence at several correctional institutions in Wisconsin. *Journal of Clinical Psychology,* 1971, *27,* 216-218.

Crano, W. D., Kenny, D. A. & Campbell, D. T. Does intelligence cause achievement? A cross-lagged panel analysis. *Journal of Educational Psychology,* 1972, *63,* 258-275.

Crites, J. O. *Vocational Psychology.* New York: McGraw-Hill, 1969.

Cronbach, L. J. The two disciplines of scientific psychology. *American Psychologist,* 1957, *12,* 671-684.

Cronbach, L. J., & Snow, R. E. *Aptitudes and instructional methods.* New York: Irvington, 1977.

Cunningham, C. H., Alston, H. L., Doughtie, E. B., & Wakefield, J. A., Jr. Use of Holland's vocational theory with potential high school dropouts. *Journal of Vocational Behavior,* 1977, *10,* 35-38.

Das, J. P., Kirby, J. & Jarmin, R. F. Simultaneous and successive synthesis: an alternative model for cognitive abilities. *Psychological Bulletin,* 1975, *82,* 87-103.

DeBoth, C. J. & Dominowski, R. L. Individual differences in learning: visual versus auditory presentation. *Journal of Educational Psychology,* 1978, *70,* 498-503.

DeFries, J. C. *et al.* Parent-offspring resemblance for specific cognitive abilities in two ethnic groups. *Nature,* 1976, *261,* 131-133.

DeFries, J. C., Vandenberg, S. G. & McClearn, G. E. Genetics of specific cognitive abilities. *Annual Review of Genetics,* 1976, *10,* 176-207.

DeGroot, A. D. War and intelligence of youth. *Journal of Abnormal and Social Psychology,* 1951, *46,* 596-597.

Delaney, H. D. Interaction of individual differences with visual and verbal elaboration instructions. *Journal of Educational Psychology,* 1978, *70,* 306-318.

Dellas, M. & Gaier, E. L. Identification of creativity: The individual. *Psychological Bulletin,* 1970, *73,* 55-73.

Doughtie, E. B., Wakefield, J. A., Jr., Sampson, R. N. & Alston, H. L. A statistical test of the theoretical model for the representational level of the ITPA. *Journal of Educational Psychology,* 1974, *66,* 410-415.

Dunteman, G. H., & Bailey, J. P., Jr. A canonical correlational analysis of the SVIB and the MMPI for a female college population. *Educational and Psychological Measurement,* 1967, *27,* 631-642.

Eaves, L. J. The structure of genotypic and environmental covariation for personality measurements: an analysis of the PEN. *British Journal of Social and Clinical Psychology,* 1973, *12,* 275-282.

Entwistle, N. J. Personality and academic attainment. *British Journal of Educational Psychology,* 1972, *42,* 137-151.

Erlenmeyer-Kimling, L., & Jarvik, L. F. Genetics and intelligence: A review. *Science,* 1963, *142,* 1477-1478.

Evans, F. J. Field dependence and the Maudsley Personality Inventory. In H. J. Eysenck (Ed.), *Reading in Extraversion-Introversion, Vol. 3.* London: Staples Press, 1971, pp. 309-310.

Eysenck, H. J. Primary mental abilities. *British Journal of Educational Psychology,* 1939, *9,* 270-275.

Eysenck, H. J. The effects of psychotherapy: an evaluation. *Journal of Consulting Psychology,* 1952, *16,* 319-324.

Eysenck, H. J. *Know your own IQ.* Baltimore: Penguin, 1962.

Eysenck, H. J. *The biological basis of personality.* Springfield, IL: Thomas, 1967.

Eysenck, H. J. *Race, intelligence and education.* London: Temple Smith, 1971.

Eysenck, H. J. *The inequality of man.* San Diego, EdITS, 1973.

Eysenck, H. J. *The measurement of personality.* Baltimore: University Park Press, 1976.

Eysenck, H. J. *The structure and measurement of intelligence.* Berlin: Springer-Verlag, 1979.

Eysenck, H. J. The place of individual differences in a scientific psychology. *Annals of Theoretical Psychology,* 1982 (in press).

Eysenck, H. J., & Eysenck, S. B. G. *Personality structure and measurement.* San Diego, EdITS, 1969.

Eysenck, H. J., & Eysenck, S. B. G. *Manual: Eysenck Personality Questionnaire (Junior and Adult).* San Diego: EdITS, 1975.

Eysenck, H. J., & Eysenck, S. B. G. *Psychoticism as a dimension of personality.* London: Hodder and Stoughton, 1976.

Eysenck, H. J., & Kamin, L. *Intelligence: The battle for the mind.* London: Pan Books, 1981.

Eysenck, H. J., & Wakefield, J. A., Jr. Psychological factors as predictors of marital satisfaction. *Advances in Behaviour Research and Therapy,* 1981, *3,* 151-192.

Eysenck, H. J., & Wilson, G. D. *The experimental study of Freudian theories.* London: Methuen, 1973.

Eysenck, H. J. & Wilson, G. D. *A textbook of human psychology.* Lancaster: Medical and Technical Publishers, 1976.

Eysenck, H. J., & Wilson, G. D. (Eds.). *The psychological basis of ideology.* Lancaster: Medical and Technical Publishers, 1978.

Eysenck, M. W., & Eysenck, H. J. Mischel and the concept of personality. *British Journal of Psychology,* 1980, *71,* 191-204.

Eysenck, S. B. G. & Eysenck, H. J. Rigidity as a function of introversion and neuroticism: a study of unmarried mothers. In H. J. Eysenck (Ed.), *Readings in Extraversion-Introversion, Vol. 2.* London: Staples Press, 1971, pp. 332-338.

Eysenck, S. B. G. & Eysenck, H. J. The place of impulsiveness in a dimensional system of personality description. *British Journal of Social and Clinical Psychology,* 1977, *16,* 57-68.

Fleishman, E. A. & Hempel, W. E., Jr. The relation between abilities and improvement with practice in a visual discrimination reaction task. *Journal of Experimental Psychology,* 1955, *49,* 301-312.

Forrest, D. W. Relationship between sharpening and extraversion. In H. J. Eysenck (Ed.), *Reading in Extraversion-Introversion, Vol. 3.* London: Staples Press, 1971, pp. 311-312.

Fraioli, R. P. Validity of response latency and accuracy on the Matching Familiar Figures Test for academic achievement. Unpublished master's thesis, California State College, Stanislaus, 1978.

Friedman, A. F., Wakefield, J. A., Jr., Boblitt, W. E., & Surman, G. Validity of psychoticism scale of the Eysenck Personality Questionnaire. *Psychological Reports,* 1976, *39,* 1309-1310.

Friedman, A. F., Wakefield, J. A., Jr., Sasek, J. & Schroeder, D. A new scoring system for the Spraings Multiple Choice Bender Gestalt Test. *Journal of Clinical Psychology,* 1977, *33,* 205-207.

Gale, A. The psychophysiology of individual differences: studies of extraversion and the EEG. In P. Kline (Ed.), *New approaches in psychological measurement.* London: Wiley, 1973, 211-256.

Galton, F. *English men of science: Their nature and nurture.* London: Macmillan, 1874.

Galton, F. *Hereditary genius.* London: Macmillan, 1925.

Gardiner, R. W., Holzman, P. S., Klein, G. S., Linton, H. B. & Spence, D. P. Cognitive control: a study of individual consistencies in cognitive behavior. *Psychological Issues,* 1959, *1* (Monograph 4).

Getzels, J. W., & Jackson, P. W. *Creativity and intelligence: Explorations with gifted students.* New York: Wiley, 1962.

Ghiselli, E. E. *The validity of occupational aptitude tests.* New York: Wiley, 1966.

Glass, G. V. Primary, secondary and meta-analysis of research. *Educational Researchers,* 1976, *5,* 3-8.

Glasser, A. J. & Zimmerman, I. L. *Clinical interpretation of the Wechsler Intelligence Scale for Children.* New York: Grune & Stratton, 1967.

Goldman, R. D., & Hewitt, B. N. The Scholastic Aptitude Test "explains" why college men major in science more often than college women. *Journal of Counseling Psychology,* 1976, *23,* 50-54.

Gottesman, I. I. Heritability of personality: A demonstration. *Psychological Monographs,* 1963, *77* (whole no. 572).

Gottfredson, L. S. Aspiration-job match: age trends in a large, nationally representative sample of young white men. *Journal of Counseling Psychology,* 1979, *26,* 319-328.

Gray, J. A. The psychophysiological basis of introversion-extraversion. *Behavior Research & Therapy,* 1970, *8,* 249-266.

Gray, J. A. The psychophysiological nature of introversion-extraversion: A modification of Eysenck's theory. In V. D. Nebylitsyn & J. A. Gray (Eds.). *The biological basis of individual behavior.* New York: Academic Press, 1972.

Guilford, J. P. *The nature of human intelligence.* New York: McGraw-Hill, 1967.

Guilford, J. P. *Cognitive psychology with a frame of reference.* San Diego: EdITS, 1979.

Guilford, J. P. Cognitive styles: What are they? *Educational and Psychological Measurement,* 1980, *40,* 715-735.

Gupta, B. S. & Nagpal, M. Impulsivity/sociability and reinforcement in verbal operant conditioning. *British Journal of Psychology,* 1978, *69,* 203-206.

Hall, J. C. Correlation of a modified form of Raven's Progressive Matrices (1938) with the WAIS. *Journal of Consulting Psychology,* 1957, *21,* 23-26.

Harman, H. H. *Modern factor analysis.* Chicago: University of Chicago Press, 1967.

Harter, S. Discrimination learning sets in children as a function of MA and IQ. *Journal of Experimental Child Psychology,* 1965, *2,* 31-43.

Hays, W. L. *Statistics.* New York: Holt, Rinehart & Winston, 1963.

Hearnshaw, L. S. *Cyril Burt, Psychologist.* Ithaca: Cornell University Press, 1979.

Hendrickson, D. E. & Hendrickson, A. E. The biological basis of individual differences in intelligence. *Personality and Individual Differences,* 1980, *1,* 3-33.

Herrnstein, R. J. *IQ in the Meritocracy,* Boston: Little, Brown, 1971.

Holder, R., & Wankowski, J. *Personality and academic performance of students at university.* Guildford, England: Society for Research into Higher Education, University of Surrey, 1980.

Holland, J. L. *Manual for the Vocational Preference Inventory.* Palo Alto, CA: Consulting Psychologists Press, 1965.

Holland, J. L. *Professional Manual for the Self-Directed Search: A guide to educational and vocational planning.* Palo Alto, CA: Consulting Psychologists Press, 1972.

Holland, J. L. *Making vocational choices: A theory of careers.* Englewood Cliffs, NJ: Prentice-Hall, 1973.

Holland, J. L. & Holland, J. E. Vocational indecision: more evidence and speculation. *Journal of Counseling Psychology,* 1977, *24,* 404-414.

Humphreys, L. G. The organization of human abilities. *American Psychologist,* 1962, *17,* 475-483.

Hunt, J. McV. *Intelligence and experience.* New York: Ronald Press, 1961.

Jencks, C., *et al. Inequality: A reassessment of the effect of family and schooling in America.* New York: Basic Books, 1972.

Jensen, A. R. How much can we boost IQ and scholastic achievement? *Harvard Educational Review,* 1969, *39,* 1-123.

Jensen, A. R. Individual differences in visual and auditory memory. *Journal of Educational Psychology,* 1971, *62,* 123-131.

Jensen, A. R. Genetic and behavioral effects of nonrandom mating. In C. E. Noble, R. T. Osborne, and N. Weyl (Eds.). *Human Variation: Biogenetics of Age, Race and Sex.* New York: Academic Press, 1977.

Jensen, A. R. *Bias in mental testing.* London: Methuen, 1980.

Kagan, J. & Kogan, N. Individual variation in cognitive processes. In P. Mussen (Ed.), *Carmichael's manual of child psychology. Vol. 1.* New York: Wiley, 1970.

Kagan, J., Moss, H. A. & Sigel, I. E. Psychological significance of styles of conceptualization. In J. C. Wright & J. Kagan (Eds.), Basic cognitive process in children. *Monographs of the Society for Research in Child Development,* 1963, *28,* (2, Serial No. 86), 73-112.

Kagan, J., Rosman, B. L., Day, D., Albert, J. & Phillips, W. Information processing in the child: significance of analytic and reflective attitudes. *Psychological Monographs,* 1964, *78,* (1, Whole No. 578).

Kamin, L. J. *The science and politics of IQ.* Potomac, MD: Lawrence Erlbaum, 1974.

Karlsson, J. L. *Inheritance of creative intelligence.* Chicago: Nelson-Hall, 1978.

Karoly, P., & Briggs, N. Z. Effects of rules and directed delays on components of children's inhibitory self-control. *Journal of Experimental Child Psychology,* 1978, *26,* 267-279.

Karp, S. Field independence and overcoming embeddedness. *Journal of Consulting Psychology,* 1963, *27,* 294-302.

Katz, M. Interests and values: A comment. *Journal of Counseling Psychology,* 1969, *16,* 460-462.

Kaufman, A. S. *Intelligent testing with the WISC-R.* New York: Wiley, 1979.

Kelly, G. A. *The psychology of personal constructs. Vol. 1.* New York: Norton, 1955.

Kerlinger, F. N. & Pedhazur, E. J. *Multiple regression in behavioral research.* New York: Holt, Rinehart & Winston, 1973.

Kirby, J. R. & Das, J. P. Information processing and human abilities. *Journal of Educational Psychology*, 1978, *70*, 58-66.

Kirk, S. A. & Kirk, W. D. *Psycholinguistic learning disabilities*. Urbana: University of Illinois Press, 1971.

Kirk, S. A., McCarthy, J. J. & Kirk, W. D. *Examiner's Manual: ITPA*. Urbana: University of Illinois Press, 1968.

Knapp, L., Knapp, R. R., Strnad, L., & Michael, W. B. Comparative validity of the Career Ability Placement Survey (CAPS) and the General Aptitude Test Battery (GATB) for predicting high school course marks. *Educational and Psychological Measurement*, 1978, *38*, 1053-1056.

Knapp, L., & Knapp, R. R. *Manual: Career Ability Placement Survey*. San Diego: EdITS, 1981.

Knapp, R. R., & Knapp, L. Relationship of work values to occupational activity interests. *Measurement and Evaluation in Guidance*, 1979, *12*, 71-76.

Knapp, R. R., & Knapp, L. *Manual: Career Orientation Placement and Evaluation Survey*. San Diego: EdITS, 1980.

Knapp, R. R., & Knapp, L. *California occupational preference system technical manual*. San Diego: EdITS, 1981.

Knapp, R. R., Knapp, L., & Buttafuoco, P. M. Interest changes and the classification of occupations. *Measurement and Evaluation in Guidance*, 1978, *11*, 14-19.

Knapp, R. R., Knapp, L., & Michael, W. B. Stability and concurrent validity of the Career Ability Placement Schedule (CAPS) against the DAT and the GATB. *Educational and Psychological Measurement*, 1977, *37*, 1081-1085.

Kogan, N. Educational implications of cognitive styles. In G. S. Lesser (Ed.), *Psychology and educational practice*. Glenview, IL: Scott, Foresman, 1971.

Kogan, N. *Cognitive styles in infancy and early childhood*. Hillsdale, NJ: Lawrence Erlbaum Associates, 1976.

Kohn, M. *Social competence, symptoms and underachievement in childhood: A longitudinal perspective*. New York: Wiley, 1977.

Lang, R. J. Multivariate classification of day-care patients: personality as a dimensional continuum. *Journal of Consulting and Clinical Psychology*, 1978, *46*, 1212-1226.

Layton, W. L. (Ed.). *The Strong Vocational Interest Blank: Research and Uses*. Minneapolis: University of Minnesota Press, 1960.

Lesser, G. S., Fifer, G. & Clark, D. H. Mental abilities of children from different social-class and cultural groups. *Monographs of the Society for Research in Child Development,* 1965, *30,* No. 4.

Lewin, L. M., & Wakefield, J. A. Jr. Percentage agreement and phi: a conversion table. *Journal of Applied Behavior Analysis,* 1979, *12,* 299-301.

Lewis, A. Attributions and politics. *Personality and Individual Differences,* 1981, *2,* 1-4.

Loehlin, J. C., Lindzey, G., & Spuhler, J. N. *Race differences in intelligence.* San Francisco: Freeman, 1975.

Loehlin, J. C. & Nichols, R. C. *Heredity, environment, and personality.* Austin: University of Texas Press, 1976.

MacKinnon, D. W. The nature and nurture of creative talent. *American Psychologist,* 1962, *17,* 484-495.

Magnusson, D., & Endler, N. S. *Personality of crossroads.* Hillsdale, NJ: Lawrence Erlbaum, 1977.

Marks, P. A., Seeman, W., & Haller, D. L. *The actuarial use of the MMPI with adolescents and adults.* Baltimore: Williams & Wilkins, 1974.

Massari, D. J. The relation of reflection-impulsivity to field dependence-independence and internal-external control in children. *Journal of Genetic Psychology,* 1975, *126,* 61-67.

Matarazzo, J. D. *Wechsler's measurement and appraisal of adult intelligence.* Baltimore: Williams & Wilkins, 1972.

Maxwell, A. E. *Multivariate analysis in behavioural research.* London: Chapman & Hall, 1977.

McClearn, G. E. & DeFries, J. C. *Introduction to behavioral genetics.* San Francisco: Freeman, 1973.

McCord, R. R., & Wakefield, J. A., Jr. Arithmetic achievement as a function of introversion-extraversion and teacher-presented reward and punishment. *Personality and Individual Differences,* 1981, *2,* 145-152.

McGee, M. G. Human spatial abilities: psychometric studies and environmental, genetic, hormonal and neurological influences. *Psychological Bulletin,* 1979, *86,* 889-918.

McNemar, Q. Lost: Our Intelligence. Why? *American Psychologist,* 1964, *19,* 871-882.

Mednick, M. T. & Andrews, F. M. Creative thinking and level of intelligence. *Journal of Creative Behavior,* 1967, *1,* 428-431.

Mednick, S. A. & Mednick, M. T. *The Remote Associates Test.* Boston: Houghton-Mifflin, 1967.

Meeker, M. *Structure of intellect: Its interpretation and uses.* Columbus, OH: Merrill, 1969.

Meeker, M. N., Mestynek, L. & Meeker, R. *SOI Learning Abilities Test: Examiner's Manual.* El Segundo, CA: SOI Institute, 1975.

Messer, S. B. Reflection-impulsivity: a review. *Psychological Bulletin,* 1976, *83,* 1026-1052.

Messick, S. Personality consistencies in cognition and creativity. In S. Messick (Ed.), *Individuality in learning.* San Francisco: Josey-Bass, 1976, pp. 4-33.

Mischel, W. On the interface of cognition and personality: Beyond the person-situation debate. *American Psychologist,* 1979, *34,* 740-754.

Mischel, W. *Personality and assessment.* London: Wiley, 1968.

Mosteller, F., & Moynihan, D. P. *On equality of educational opportunity.* New York: Random House, 1972.

Naylor, F. D. *Personality and educational achievement.* Sydney: Wiley, 1972.

Naylor, H. Reading disability and lateral asymmetry: an information processing analysis. *Psychological Bulletin,* 1980, *87,* 531-545.

Oden, M. H. The fulfillment of promise: 40-year follow-up of the Terman gifted group. *Genetic Psychology Monographs,* 1968, *77,* 3-93.

O'Neil, J. M., Magoon, T. M. & Tracey, T. J. Status of Holland's investigative personality types and their consistency levels seven years later. *Journal of Counseling Psychology,* 1978, *25,* 530-535.

Osborn, A. F. *Applied imagination.* New York: Scribner's, 1953.

Osborne, R. T. *Twins: black and white.* Athens, GA: Foundation for Human Understanding, 1980.

Osipow, S. H. Cognitive styles and educational-vocational preferences and selection. *Journal of Counseling Psychology,* 1969, *16,* 534-546.

Osipow, S. H., Ashby, J. D., & Wall, H. W. Personality types and vocational choice: a test of Holland's theory. *Personnel and Guidance Journal,* 1966, *45,* 37-42.

Packer, J. & Bain, J. D. Cognitive style and teacher-student compatibility. *Journal of Educational Psychology,* 1978, *70,* 864-871.

Paivio, A. *Imagery and verbal processes.* New York: Holt, Rinehart & Winston, 1971.

Pearlman, K. Job families: a review and discussion of their implications for personnel selections. *Psychological Bulletin,* 1980, *87,* 1-28.

Pettigrew, T. F. The measurement and correlation of category width as a cognitive variable. *Journal of Personality,* 1958, *26,* 532-544.

Phillips, B. N. *School stress and anxiety.* New York: Human Sciences Press, 1978.

Rahman, M. A., & Eysenck, S. B. G. Psychoticism and response to treatment in neurotic patients. *Behaviour Research and Therapy,* 1978, *16,* 183-189.

Riding, R. J., & Dyer, V. A. The relationship between extraversion and verbal-imagery learning style in twelve year old children. *Personality and Individual Differences.* 1980, *1,* 273-279.

Roe, A. *The psychology of occupations.* New York: Wiley, 1956.

Roe, A. & Klos, D. Occupational classification. *Counseling Psychologist,* 1969.

Rogers, C. R. Toward a theory of creativity. In H. H. Anderson, (Ed.), *Creativity and its cultivation.* New York: Harper, 1959.

Sattler, J. M. *Assessment of children's intelligence.* Philadelphia: Saunders, 1974.

Scarr-Salapatek, S. Race, social class and IQ. *Science,* 1971, *174,* 1285-1295.

Schneider, L. J., DeWinne, R. F., & Overton, T. D. Influence of congruity between parental personality types on offspring's personality development. *Journal of Counseling Psychology,* 1980, *27,* 40-43.

Schuerger, J. M. & Watterson, D. G. *Using tests and other information in counseling.* Champaign, IL: Institute for Personality and Ability Testing, 1977.

Skodak, M. & Skeels, H. M. A follow-up study of children in adoptive homes. *Journal of Genetic Psychology,* 1945, *66,* 21-58.

Skodak, M. & Skeels, H. M. A final follow-up study of one hundred adopted children. *Journal of Genetic Psychology,* 1949, *75,* 85-125.

Spearman, C. "General intelligence," objectively determined and measured. *American Journal of Psychology,* 1904, *15,* 201-293.

Spearman, C. *The abilities of man.* London: Macmillan, 1927.

Sperry, R. W. Hemispheric deconnection and unity in conscious awareness. *American Psychologist,* 1968, *23,* 723-733.

Spokane, A. R. Occupational preference and the validity of the Strong-Campbell Interest Inventory for college women and men. *Journal of Counseling Psychology,* 1979, *26,* 312-318.

Strong, E. K. *Vocational interests of men and women.* Palo Alto, CA: Stanford University Press, 1943.

Taylor, C. W., & Barron, F. *Scientific creativity: Its recognition and development.* New York: Wiley, 1963.

Taylor, C. W., & Holland, J. Predictors of creative performance. In C. W. Taylor (Ed.), *Creativity: Progress and potential.* New York: McGraw-Hill, 1964.

Terman, L. M. & Merrill, M. A. *Stanford-Binet Intelligence Scale.* Cambridge, MA: Houghton Mifflin, 1960.

Terman, L. M. *et al. Mental and Physical Traits of a Thousand Gifted Children.* Stanford, CA: Stanford University Press, 1925.

Terman, L. M. & Oden, M. H. *The Gifted Child Grows Up: Twenty-five Years Follow-up of a Superior Group.* Stanford, CA: Stanford University Press, 1947.

Terman, L. M. & Oden, M. H. *The Gifted Group at Mid-Life.* Stanford, CA: Stanford University Press, 1959.

Testo, M. P. The relationship of reflection-impulsivity to reading recognition, reading comprehension, arithmetic, and spelling. Unpublished master's thesis, California State College, Stanislaus, 1979.

Tharp, R. G. & Wetzel, R. J. *Behavior modification in the natural environment.* New York: Academic Press, 1969.

Thompson, B., Alston, H. L., Cunningham, C. H. & Wakefield, J. A., Jr. The relationship of a measure of structure of intellect abilities and academic achievement. *Educational and Psychological Measurement,* 1978, *38,* 1207-1210.

Thomson, G. H. *The factorial analysis of human ability.* London: University of London Press, 1941.

Thorndike, R., Weiss, D., & Dawis, R. Canonical correlation of vocational interests and vocational needs. *Journal of Counseling Psychology,* 1968, *15,* 101-106.

Thurstone, L. L. & Thurstone, T. G. *Factorial studies of intelligence.* Chicago: University of Chicago Press, 1941.

Torrance, E. P. *Guiding creative talent.* Englewood Cliffs, NJ: Prentice-Hall, 1962.

Vernon, P. E. *Personality tests and assessments.* London: Methuen, 1953.

Vernon, P. E. *The structure of human abilities* (2nd ed.). London: Methuen, 1961.

Vernon, P. E. Multivariate approaches to the study of cognitive styles. In J. R. Royce (Ed.), *Multivariate analysis and psychological theory.* New York: Academic Press, 1973. Pp. 125-144.

Vernon, P. E. *Intelligence: Heredity and Environment.* San Francisco: Freeman, 1979.

Wachtel, P. L. Style and capacity in analytic functioning. *Journal of Personality,* 1968, *36,* 202-212.

Wakefield, J. A., Jr. *Using personality to individualize instruction.* San Diego: EdITS, 1979.

Wakefield, J. A., Jr. Relationship between two expressions of reliability: percentage agreement and phi. *Educational and Psychological Measurement,* 1980, *40,* 593-597.

Wakefield, J. A., Jr., Alston, H. L., Yom, B. L., & Doughtie, E. B. Related factors of the Survey of Study Habits and Attitudes and the Vocational Preference Inventory. *Journal of Vocational Behavior,* 1974, *5,* 215-219.

Wakefield, J. A., Jr., Bradley, P. E., Doughtie, E. B., & Kraft, I. A. Influence of overlapping and non-overlapping items on the theoretical interrelationships of MMPI scales. *Journal of Consulting and Clinical Psychology,* 1975, *43,* 851-857.

Wakefield, J. A., Jr., & Carlson, R. E. Canonical analysis of the WISC and the ITPA. *Psychology in the Schools,* 1975, *12,* 18-20.

Wakefield, J. A., Jr., & Cunningham, C. H. Relationships between the Vocational Preference Inventory and the Edwards Personal Preferences Schedule. *Journal of Vocational Behavior,* 1975, *6,* 373-377.

Wakefield, J. A., Jr., Cunningham, C. H., & Edwards, D. D. Teacher attitudes and personality. *Psychology in the Schools,* 1975, *12,* 345-347.

Wakefield, J. A., Jr., & Doughtie, E. B. The geometic relationship between Holland's personality typology and the Vocational Preference Inventory. *Journal of Counseling Psychology,* 1973, *20,* 513-518.

Wakefield, J. A., Jr., & Goad, N. A. Creativity, personality, and intelligence. *Creative Child and Adult Quarterly,* 1981, *6,* 13-18.

Wakefield, J. A., Jr., Yom, B. L., Bradley, P. E., Doughtie, E. B., Cox, J. A., & Kraft, I. A. Eysenck's personality dimensions: A model for the MMPI. *British Journal of Social and Clinical Psychology,* 1974, *13,* 413-420.

Wakefield, J. A., Jr., Yom, B. L., Doughtie, E. B., Chang, W. C., & Alson, H. L. The geometric relationship between Holland's personality typology and the Vocational Preferences Inventory for blacks. *Journal of Counseling Psychology,* 1975, *22,* 58-60.

Wallas, G. *The art of thought.* New York: Harcourt, Brace, 1926.

Walsh, W. B. Consistent occupational preferences and personality. *Journal of Vocational Behavior,* 1974, *4,* 145-153.

Ward, G. R., Cunningham, C. H., & Wakefield, J. A., Jr. Relationships between Holland's VPI and Cattell's 16 PF. *Journal of Vocational Behavior,* 1976, *8,* 307-312.

Wardell, D. M. & Royce, J. R. Toward a multifactor theory of styles and their relationships to cognition and affect. *Journal of Personality,* 1978, *46,* 474-505.

Wechsler, D. *Wechsler Adult Intelligence Scale - Revised.* New York: Psychological Corp., 1980.

Wechsler, D. *Wechsler Intelligence Scale for Children - Revised.* New York: Psychological Corp., 1974.

Wechsler, D. *Wechsler Preschool and Primary Scale of Intelligence.* New York: Psychological Corp., 1967.

Weil, P. G. Influence du milieu sur le developpement mental. *Enfance,* 1958, *2,* 151-160.

Welsh, G. S. *Creativity and intelligence: A personality approach.* Chapel Hill, NC: Institute for Research in Social Science, University of North Carolina, 1975.

Wesley, S. M., Corey, D. Q. & Stewart, M. The intra-individual relationship between interest and ability. *Journal of Applied Psychology,* 1950, *34,* 193-197.

Wiens, A. N., & Banaka, W. H. Estimating WAIS IQ from Shipley-Hartford scores. *Journal of Clinical Psychology,* 1960, *16,* 452.

Wiggins, J. S. *Personality and prediction.* Reading, MA: Addison-Wesley, 1973.

Willerman, L. *The psychology of individual and group differences.* San Francisco: Freeman, 1979.

Wilson, G. Introversion/extraversion. In H. London and J. Exner, Jr. (Eds.). *Dimensions of Personality.* New York: Wiley, 1978, pp. 217-261.

Witkin, H. A. Cognitive style in academic performance and in teacher-student selections. In S. Messick (Ed.), *Individuality in learning.* San Francisco: Jossey-Bass, 1976, pp. 38-72.

Witkin, H. A. & Goodenough, D. R. Field dependence and interpersonal behavior. *Psychological Bulletin,* 1977, *84,* 661-689.

Witkin, H. A., Lewis, H. B., Hertzmann, M., Machover, K., Meissner, P. B. & Wapner, S. *Personality through perception.* New York: Harper & Row, 1954.

Witkin, H. A., Moore, C. A., Goodenough, D. R., & Cox, P. W. Field dependent and field independent cognitive styles and their educational implications. *Review of Educational Research,* 1977, *47,* 1-64.

Woody, E., & Claridge, G. Psychoticism and thinking, *British Journal of Social and Clinical Psychology,* 1977, *16,* 241-248.

Yamamoto, K. Effects of restriction of range and test unreliability on correlation between measures of intelligence and creative thinking. *British Journal of Educational Psychology,* 1965, *35,* 300-305.

Yom, B. L., Bradley, P. E., Wakefield, J. A., Jr., Kraft, I. A. Doughtie, E. G., & Cox, J. A. A common factor in the MMPI scales of married couples. *Journal of Personality Assessment,* 1975, *39,* 64-69.

Yom, B. L., Wakefield, J. A., Jr., & Doughtie, E. G. The psycholinguistic and conservation abilities of five-year-old children. *Psychology in the Schools,* 1975, *12,* 150-152.

Zajonc, R. B. & Markus, G. B. Birth order and intellectual development. *Psychological Review,* 1975, *82,* 74-88.

Zytowski, D. G. Predictive validity of the Kuder Occupational Interest Survey: a 12- to 19-year follow-up. *Journal of Counseling Psychology,* 1975, *23,* 221-233.

AUTHOR INDEX

SUBJECT INDEX